Head of Gorgon, from the Pediment of the Temple of
Svl Minerva at Bath ($\frac{1}{7}$). See page 53.

THE

ROMANIZATION

OF

ROMAN BRITAIN

BY

F. HAVERFIELD

———◆———

FOURTH EDITION

revised by

GEORGE MACDONALD

GREENWOOD PRESS, PUBLISHERS
WESTPORT, CONNECTICUT

Library of Congress Cataloging in Publication Data

Haverfield, Francis John, 1860-1919.
   The Romanization of Roman Britain.

   Reprint of the ed. published at the Clarendon Press,
Oxford.
   Includes bibliographical references and index.
   1. Great Britain--Antiquities, Roman. 2. Romans--
Great Britain. I. Macdonald, George, Sir, 1862-1940.
II. Title.
DA145.H3 1979   936.2   78-12798
ISBN 0-313-21148-5

Reprinted in 1979 by Greenwood Press, Inc.,
51 Riverside Avenue, Westport, CT 06880

Printed in the United States of America

10 9 8 7 6 5 4 3 2 1

PREFATORY NOTE

THIS Essay was originally published in 1906. It was re-issued in 1912 and again in 1915, undergoing on each occasion a very considerable enlargement. A fourth edition has now been called for. *Inter arma* but little fresh material has accumulated. In the circumstances it may be doubted whether the author would have felt that any extensive re-casting was desirable. But he would certainly not have been satisfied with a literal reprint. In point of fact he had made a few jottings as to possible improvements. The present edition gives effect to his wishes for amendment. Beyond this, all that has been done is to introduce into text and foot-notes such modifications and additions as seemed to be necessary, if the whole was to be brought up to date. The number of illustrations has been increased by one.

Thanks for help and advice are due to several of Professor Haverfield's friends, notably Miss M. V. Taylor and Mr. W. H. Stevenson.   G. M.

EDINBURGH,
June, 1922.

FROM THE PREFACE TO THE THIRD EDITION

THE following pages are based on a paper which I read to the British Academy in 1905 and which, according to the custom of the Academy, was issued both in its general ' Proceedings ' (ii. 185–217) and separately. In its separate form it soon ran out of print, and in 1912 the Delegates of the Clarendon Press published a new edition, revised and enlarged to about twice its original size. This second edition is now in turn exhausted ; in issuing a third, I have revised and in places recast the text, and I have again increased considerably both text and illustrations. I have tried to preserve the character of the work as a treatise on a definite subject which seems to possess quite real interest and importance ; I have also endeavoured so to word my matter that the text, though not the footnotes, can be read easily by any one who is interested in the subject, without special knowledge of Latin.

CONTENTS

CHAP.   PAGE

    LIST OF ILLUSTRATIONS 7

1. THE ROMANIZATION OF THE EMPIRE . . . 9

2. PRELIMINARY REMARKS ON ROMAN BRITAIN . 23

3. ROMANIZATION OF BRITAIN IN LANGUAGE . . 29

4. ROMANIZATION IN MATERIAL CIVILIZATION . . 36

5. ROMANIZATION IN ART 48

6. ROMANIZATION IN TOWN-LIFE, LOCAL GOVERN-
    MENT AND LAND-TENURE 57

7. ROMANIZATION IN RELIGION · 67

8. CHRONOLOGY OF THE ROMANIZATION . . . 74

9. THE SEQUEL, THE CELTIC REVIVAL IN THE LATER
    EMPIRE 80

    INDEX 89

LIST OF ILLUSTRATIONS

FIG.   PAGE

Head of Gorgon from Bath. (*From a photo-graph*) . . . . . . *Frontispiece*

1. The Civil and Military Districts of Britain . . 25

2, 3, and 4. Inscribed tiles from Silchester. (*From photographs*) . . . . . *facing p.* 30

5. Inscribed tile from Silchester. (*From a drawing by Sir E. M. Thompson*). 30

6. Reconstruction of the Plaxtol Inscription from various fragments 33

7. Inscribed tile from Plaxtol, Kent. (*From a photo-graph*) . . . . . . *facing p.* 33

8. Fragment of inscribed jar, from Ickleton. (*From a photograph*) . . . . *facing p.* 33

9. Ground-plans of Romano-British Temples. (*From Archaeologia*) 37

10A. Ground-plan of House at Brislington . . 38

10B. Ground-plan of House at Clanville. (*From Archaeo-logia*) 38

11. Plan of House at Frilford 39

12. Ground-plan of Courtyard House at Northleigh . 41

13. Plan of a part of Silchester, showing private houses, the Forum, and the Christian Church. (*From Archaeologia*) 43

14. Painted pattern on wall-plaster from Silchester. (*Restoration by G. E. Fox, Archaeologia*) *facing p.* 44

15. Plan of British Village at Din Lligwy. (*From Archaeologia Cambrensis*) 47

16. Late Celtic Metal Work. (*From a photograph*) *facing p.* 48

FIG.   PAGE

17. Fragments of New Forest pottery with leaf patterns. (*From Archaeologia*) .   .   .   49

18. Castor Ware. (*From photographs*) . *facing p.*   50

19. Hunting Scenes from Castor Ware. (*From Artis, Durobrivae*) .   .   .   .   . *facing p.*   50

20. Fragment of Castor Ware showing Hercules and Hesione. (*After C. R. Smith*)   51

21. Bow-Fibula. (*From a drawing by O. Jewitt*) . 52

22. Dragon-brooches. (*From a drawing by C. J. Praetorius*)   52

23. The Corbridge Lion. (*From a photograph*) *facing p.*   53

24. Inscription from Caerwent, illustrating cantonal government. (*From a drawing*) .   .   .   59

25. Plan of Silchester. (*From the author's ' Ancient Town-planning '*, Fig. 31)   63

26. Relief of Diana and Hound from Nettleton. (*From a photograph*) .   .   .   . *facing p.*   73

27. Relief of Mercury and Rosmerta from Gloucester. (*From a photograph*) .   .   . *facing p.*   73

28. Ogam inscription from Silchester. (*From a drawing by C. J. Praetorius, Archaeologia*) .   .   .   82

Note. For the blocks of the frontispiece and of Figs. 3, 5, 18, 19, I am indebted to the editor and publishers of the Victoria County History. For the block of Fig. 13 I have to thank the Royal Institute of British Architects. The block of Fig. 26 has been kindly lent by the Bath Branch of the Somersetshire Archaeological Society.

CHAPTER I

The Romanization of the Empire

HISTORIANS seldom praise the Roman Empire. They regard it as a period of death and despotism, from which manly vigour and political freedom and creative genius and the energies of the speculative intellect were all alike excluded. There is, unquestionably, much truth in this judgement. The world of the Empire was indeed, as Mommsen has called it, an old world. Behind it lay the dreams and experiments, the self-convicted follies and disillusioned wisdom of many centuries. Before it lay no untravelled region such as revealed itself to our forefathers at the Renaissance or to our fathers fifty years ago. No new continent then rose up beyond the western seas. No forgotten literature suddenly flashed out its long-lost splendours. No vast discoveries of science transformed the universe and the interpretation of it. The inventive freshness and intellectual confidence that are born of such things were denied to the Empire. Its temperament was neither artistic, nor literary, nor scientific. It was merely practical.

Yet, if practical, it was not therefore uncreative. Within its own sphere of everyday life, it was an epoch of growth in many directions. Even art moved forward. Sculpture was enriched by a new and noble style of portraiture and by a school of historical narrative in stone. Architecture found new possibilities in the aqueduct of Segovia and the Basilica of Maxentius.[1] But it was only practical ends—the erection of buildings or the historical representation of men and deeds—that woke the artistic powers of the Romans. The greatest work of the imperial age must be sought in its

---

[1] Wickhoff, *Wiener Genesis*, p. 10 ; Riegl, *Stilfragen*, p. 272.

provincial administration.   The significance of this we have come to understand, as not even Gibbon understood it, through the researches of Mommsen.   By his vast labours our horizon has broadened beyond the backstairs of the Palace and the benches of the Senate House in Rome to the wide lands north and east and south of the Mediterranean, and we have begun to realize the true achievements of the Empire.   The old theory of an age of despotism and decay has been overthrown, and the believer in human nature can now feel confident that, whatever their limitations, the men of the Empire wrought for the betterment and the happiness of the world.

Their efforts took two forms.   They defended the frontiers against the barbarians and secured internal peace; they developed the civilization of the provinces during that peace.   The first of these achievements was but for a time. In the end the Roman legionary went down before the Gothic horseman.   The barbarians were many ;[1] they were also formidable fighters ;   perhaps, without railways and explosives, no generalship could have wholly kept them back.   But they won no rapid entrance.   From the middle of the second century, when their assaults became violent, two hundred years passed before they won a real footing, and the Roman lines were still held in some fashion even in the beginning of the fifth century.   Despotism did not destroy, nor ease steal away, the manly vigour of the Empire. Through battles without and tumults within, through the red carnage of uncounted wars, through the devastations of great plagues, through civil discord and sedition and domestic treachery, the work went on.   It was not always marked by special insight or intelligence.   The men who carried it out were not for the most part first-rate statesmen or first-rate generals.   Even in the art of war they were slow to learn ;   they clung to an obsolete infantry, they neglected

---

[1] Some recent writers, like Dubois in *Mélanges Cagnat*, pp. 247–67, try to minimize their numbers, but they do not seem to me quite to prove their case.

new tactics and new engines. Their successes were those of character, not of genius. But their phlegmatic courage saved the Empire through many years and secured for the lands within the frontiers an almost unbroken quiet. The age of the Empire is the longest interval—indeed, it is the one long interval—of peace which has yet been granted to any large portion of our world.

The long peace made possible the second and more lasting achievement of the Empire. The lands which the legions sheltered were not merely blessed with quiet. They were also given a civilization, and that civilization had time to take strong root. Roman speech and manners were diffused ; the political franchise was extended ; city life was established ; the provincial populations were assimilated in an orderly and coherent culture. A large part of the world became Romanized. The fact has an importance which, even to-day, we might easily miss. It is not likely that any modern nation will soon stand in quite the place which Rome then held. Our civilization seems firmly set in many lands ; our task is rather to spread it further and develop its good qualities than to defend its life. If war destroy it in one continent, it has other homes. But the Roman Empire was the civilized world ; the safety of Rome was the safety of all civilization. Outside roared the wild chaos of barbarism. Rome kept it back, from end to end of Europe and across a thousand miles of western Asia. Had Rome failed to civilize, had the civilized life found no period in which to grow firm and tenacious, civilization would have perished utterly. The culture of the old world would not have lived on, to form the groundwork of the best culture of to-day.

The Empire did not, of course, grow into a nation, in the sense in which we now use that word. It resembled Austria, as it was before the peace of Versailles, rather than France or Germany. But it gained—what Austria missed—a unity of sentiment and culture which served some of the purposes of national feeling. Late in its days, about A.D. 400, a Greek from Egypt, who was also the last great Latin poet, wrote

a remarkable praise of Rome. She (he sang) alone of conquerors had taken to her bosom the world which she had
subdued ; she had been mother, not mistress, and to her men
owed it that from Rhone to Orontes—from the Atlantic to the
sands of the Arabian desert—they were all one people.[1]
Claudian was probably echoing here an earlier Greek littéra-
teur. But that neither makes him insincere nor his words
untrue. He felt, and felt rightly, that Romanization was
a real thing. The Empire had passed out beyond the nar-
rower ideal of military dominion, which at its birth Vergil had
set forth in famous verses.[2] Rulers and ruled had assimilated;
a civilized life had grown up which even its barbarian
assailants learnt to honour and accept and which they passed
on to later ages.

This Romanization was real. But it was, necessarily, not
altogether uniform and monotonous throughout all the wide
Roman lands. Its methods of development and its fruits
varied with local conditions, with racial and geographical
differences. It had its limits and its characteristics. First,
in respect of place. Not only in the further east, where (as
in Egypt) mankind was non-European, but even in the nearer
east, where an ancient Greek civilization reigned, the effect
of Romanization was inevitably small. Closely as Greek
civilization resembled Roman, easy as the transition might
seem from the one to the other, Rome met here that most
serious of all obstacles to union, a race whose thoughts and
affections and traditions had crystallized into definite coherent form. That has in all ages checked Imperial assimila-
tion ; it was the decisive hindrance to the full Romanization
of the Greek east. A few Italian oases were created by
the establishment of *coloniae* here and there in Asia Minor
and in Syria. Such, for example, were Alexandria Troas, close
by ancient Troy, or Antioch in Pisidia, explored in 1912–13

---

[1] *Quod cuncti gens una sumus*, Claudian, *de cons. Stilichonis*, iii.
150–9. The idea seems taken from Aelius Aristides, who in his
' Praise of Rome ' called her πάντων μήτηρ and speaks of the Empire as
μία χώρα συνεχὴς καὶ ἓν φῦλον : he wrote in the middle of the second
century.

[2] *Aen.* vi. 847 foll. *tu regere imperio populos*, etc. See *Some Roman
Conceptions of Empire* (Occasional Publications of the Classical Associa-
tion, No. 4), 10 ff.

by Sir W. M. Ramsay, or Berytus on the Syrian coast. The colonists, the speech, the constitutions of these settlements were Roman, and now and again their citizens won high office at Rome. From Troas, to quote one case only, came the Quintilii who held four consulships in the later second century and who dwelt in the largest of all the palaces in the Campagna of Rome. But in one after another of these towns the Roman element perished like an exotic plant.[1] The Romanization of these lands was political. Their inhabitants learnt to call and to deem themselves Romans. They did not adopt the Roman language or much of the Roman civilization.

The west offers a different spectacle. Here Rome found *— Britain* races that were not yet civilized, yet were racially capable of accepting her culture. Here, accordingly, her conquests differed from the two forms of conquest with which modern men are most familiar. We know well enough the rule of civilized white men over uncivilized Africans, who seem sundered for ever from their conquerors by a broad physical distinction. We know, too, the rule of civilized white men over civilized white men—of Prussian (for example) over Pole, where the individualities of two civilized races have for generations clashed in undying conflict. The Roman conquest of western Europe resembled neither of these. , Celt, Iberian, German, Illyrian, were marked off from Italian by no broad distinction of race and colour, such as that which marked off the ancient Egyptian from the Italian, or that which now divides the Frenchman from the Algerian Arab. They were marked off, further, by no ancient culture, such as that which had existed for centuries round the Aegean. It was possible, it was easy, to Romanize these western peoples.

---

[1] Mitteis, *Reichsrecht und Volksrecht*, p. 147 ; Kubitschek, *Festheft Bormann* (Wiener Studien, xx. 2), pp. 340 foll. ; L. Hahn, *Rom und Romanismus im griechisch-röm. Osten* (Leipzig, 1906). One reason for the loss of Roman culture is indicated by inscriptions like C.I.L. iii. 6800 (from the interior of Asia Minor), on which a veteran of Legio xii Fulminata commemorates a wife with the purely native name of Ba. This legionary must have had some knowledge of the Latin language and the Roman civilization : his children probably had none.

Even their geographical position helped somewhat indirectly to further the process. Tacitus two or three times observes that the western provinces of the Empire looked out on no other land to the westward and bordered on no free nations. That is one half of a larger fact which influenced the whole history of the Empire. Round the west lay the sea and the Sahara. In the east were wide lands and powerful states and military dangers and political problems and commercial opportunities. The Empire arose in the west and in Italy, a land that, geographically speaking, looks westward. But it was drawn surely, if slowly, to the east. Throughout the first three centuries of our era, we can trace an eastward drift—of troops, of officials, of government machinery—till finally the capital itself is no longer Rome but Byzantium. All the while, in the undisturbed security of the west, Romanization proceeded steadily.

The advance of this Romanization followed manifold lines. Much was due to official encouragement by statesmen who cherished the ideal of assimilating the provinces or who recognized more cynically that civilized men are easier ruled than savages.[1] More, perhaps, was spontaneous. The definite and coherent culture of Rome took hold on uncivilized but intelligent provincials and planted in them the wish to learn its language and share its benefits. And this wish was all the keener since Roman tolerance drove no one into uniformity. The compulsion to accept another speech and another nationality which has been laid at one time or another on Slav or Magyar or Alsatian French in modern Europe—always with unsuccess—was no part of Roman policy. Rome made her culture more attractive by not thrusting it upon her subjects.

The most potent single factor in the Romanization was the town. Italian civilization was itself based on city life;

---

[1] Tacitus (*Agr.* 21) emphasizes this : *ut homines dispersi ac rudes, eoque in bella faciles, quieti et otio per voluptates adsuescerent, hortari privatim adiuvare publice ut templa fora domos exstruerent. . . . Idque apud imperitos humanitas vocabatur, cum pars servitutis esset.*

it was natural that the Empire should diffuse that life, especially in the provinces of western and central Europe which had few towns or none before they came under Roman rule. The most common step in this direction, at least in the early Empire, was the foundation of *coloniae*, municipalities on the Italian pattern, manned by time-expired legionaries (men who were citizens of Rome and spoke Latin [1]), laid out on Roman town-plans,[2] decorated with Roman street-names and in all essentials Roman cities. These *coloniae* were not meant altogether as missionaries of culture. Primarily, they served as informal fortresses. When Cicero [3] describes one of them, founded under the Republic in southern Gaul, as ' a watchtower of the Roman people and its outpost against the tribes of Gaul ', he states an aspect of such a town which obtained during the first century of the Empire no less than in the Republican age. Nevertheless, they inevitably became centres of Roman life, and though, being somewhat artificial military creations, they were liable, as in the east (p. 13), to be gradually merged in the peoples round them,[4] most of them escaped this fate and really helped in Romanization.

Other towns were less direct official creations. Often, native provincial markets or other centres of life grew so far Romanized that they were held to merit the rights and status of a Roman municipality, and the wisdom of the Roman government in recognizing such progress was well repaid by the development of fresh centres of Roman civilization. Often, the legionary fortresses attracted traders, women, veterans and others to settle outside their gates but under the shelter of their ramparts, and their *canabae*,

---

[1] Till about A.D. 70 most of the legionaries were Italians ; later, they were recruited in the provinces but they regularly came from towns which were adequately Romanized. Tiberius *militem Graece testimonium interrogatum nisi Latine respondere vetuit* (Suet. *Tib.* 71).

[2] I m y refer to my *Ancient Town-planning* (Oxford, 1913), ch. viii.

[3] *Pro Fonteio* 13. So Tac. *Ann.* xii. 27 and 31, *Agr.* 14 and 32.

[4] Even Colonia Agrippinensis (Cologne) on the Rhine nearly fell victim to this at one moment, Tac. *Hist.* iv. 65.

or ' bazaars ', to use an Anglo-Indian term, grew not seldom into cities, worthy of municipal position. No doubt in all these towns it was the municipal aristocracies which were especially Roman. Like the German municipal elements in mediaeval Cracow and elsewhere in eastern Europe, they rested on a stratum which was less civilized. Yet we shall see below that in many provincial Roman towns even the lower stratum was Roman or Romanized.

Towns were not the only factors in the process. Provincials who seemed ripe for it often received grants of the franchise individually or in large bodies. The abler provincials who became Romanized found careers open to them at Rome. Everywhere was practical inducement for the native to enlist in the Roman culture. Weight, too, must be ascribed to the drift of Italians into the provinces. This was not a population-making emigration, like the present-day mass emigrations of the Italian lower classes. It was rather a drift of men from the well-to-do middle classes, merchants and others, who formed little Roman centres where neither troops nor Roman municipalities existed.[1] It was just such an emigration as that by which mediaeval Germans helped to civilize parts of Galicia and Hungary and to diffuse some sort of town-life through them.[2]   If it did not Romanize on the lines along which we have Anglicized Australia, it was still a strong culture-making force. It added its aid to the spread of town-life and to the willingness of the provincial to carry Romanization through.[3]

The process is hard to follow chronologically, since datable evidence is scanty. In general, however, the instances of really native fashions or speech which are recorded from this or that province belong to the early Empire. To that age

---

[1] Schulten, *de conventibus civium romanorum* ; Kornemann, *de civibus rom. in provinciis imperii consistentibus*. For an example take an inscription from Bourges in Aquitania, *pro salute Caesarum et p. R., Minervae et divae Drusillae sacrum in perpetuum, C. Agileius Primus vi. vir Aug., c(urator) c(ivium) r(omanorum)*, dating from A.D. 38–40 (C.I.L. xiii (1) 1194).

[2] R. F. Kaindl, *Geschichte der Deutschen in den Karpathenländern.*

[3] On the influence of the *negotiatores* see Cumont, *Belgique romanisée*, pp. 21–4.

we can assign the Celtic, Iberian, and Punic inscriptions
which occur occasionally in Gaul, Spain, and Africa, the
strange sculptures of three-headed or horned or cross-legged
deities in northern Gaul, the use of native titles like Ver-
gobret or Suffete, and the retention of native personal names
and of that class of Latin *nomina*, like Lovessius, which are
formed out of native names.

In the second and third centuries of the Empire there is
a change. Roman elements now dominate ; in most regions
native survivals are few. But they are not merely few ;
they no longer stand out in hostile contrast with the Roman
civilization. The two have harmonized ; amalgamation has
gone forward. Indeed, one province can show from this age
a few native items unknown in earlier days of Roman rule.
In Gaul, or rather in some districts of that large area, the
Celtic measure of distance, the ' leuga ' of about 2,500 yards,
appears on official milestones in place of the Roman *mille
passus*,[1] while the Druids, banned by the first Emperors,
emerge from their hiding, though in very humble fashion.
But these things are plainly not due to anti-Roman or even
un-Roman feeling. The real position can be seen best in the
curious 'Gallic Empire' of A. D. 258–73.[2] Here Roman elements
dominated, but they mixed in friendly fashion with native
things. The emperors of this state were called not only
Latinius Postumus, but also Piavonius and Esuvius Tetricus.
Its coins were inscribed not only ' Romae Aeternae ' and
' Spei Publicae ', but also ' Herculi Deusoniensi ' and
' Herculi Magusano '. It not only claimed independence
of Rome, but it modelled itself on Rome. It had its own
senate and consuls ; just as at Rome, *tribunicia potestas* was
conferred on its ruler, and the title *princeps iuventutis* on its
heir-apparent. We see Gaulish rulers with Gaulish names
appealing in some sort to native memories and at the same

---

[1] The ' leuga ' does not occur in the first century ; in the second it
displaced the Roman measure in certain districts, and later it was used
still more freely. But it never got into Gallia Narbonensis.

[2] An admirable account of this has recently been given by M. Camille
Jullian in his *Histoire de la Gaule*, iv. 570–92.

moment fully accepting Roman fashions, speech and political institutions. The native element in Gaul had not quite died out of mind, but it had become little more than a picturesque contrast to the Roman. If this Gallic Empire in some details recalls the past, it still more looks forward. Its independence, its cry of ' Gaul for the Gauls ', is a geographical fact, not a racial survival. It demanded individual life, and doubtless also individual protection from the barbarians, for a Roman section of the Roman world. It anticipated the birth of new nations.

Progress in Romanization was perhaps slowest in language, especially in the remoter districts of the Empire. In Roman Africa, Punic was in almost official use in towns like Gigthis, in the Syrtis, as late as the second century, and Punic-speaking clergy were needed in outlying villages even in the fourth century. In Gaul, Celtic is stated [1] to have been spoken at the same epoch among the Treveri, who lived round what is now Trier. Presumably the native idiom lingered on in the vast woodlands of the Eifel and Hunsrück and Ardennes and in the hills above the upper Mosel valley, from which uncouth uplanders came down to sell forest-produce in towns, where they must have looked as strange as the Górals of to-day in the streets of Cracow or Lemberg. On the borders of Gaul and Spain, in the shadowy valleys of the Pyrenees, Basque must have survived throughout the Roman age, as it has done ever since. On the high plateau of Asia Minor, where Greek was the dominant tongue of civilized folk, six or seven other dialects, Galatian, Phrygian, Lycaonian, and the rest, lived on till a very late date, especially (as it seems) on the wild and remote pastures of the Imperial domain-lands.[2] Some of these are survivals, noted

[1] Jerome, *comment. in epist. ad Galatas*, ii. 3. He is the only authority and his accuracy has been doubted. But other survivals can be quoted from this region ; here, for instance, in the secluded region of Birkenfeld, the Celto-Roman culture is said to have resisted Germanization long after the lowlands had succumbed. (Cumont, *Belgique romanisée*, p. 95, takes the same view as I have given above.)

[2] K. Holl, *Hermes*, xliii. 240–54 ; W. M. Ramsay, *Oesterr. Jahreshefte*, viii (1905), 79–120, quoting, amongst other things, a neophrygian text of A.D. 259 ; W. M. Calder, *Hellenic Journal*, xxxi. 161.

at the time as exceptional, and counting in the scales of history for no more than the survival of Croatian in a few villages of the Italian Abruzzi or of Wendish (Sorb) fifty miles from Berlin. Others are more serious facts. But they do not alter the main position. In most regions of the west the Latin tongue obviously prevailed.[1] It was, indeed, powerful enough to lead the Christian Church to insist on its use, and not, as in Syria and Egypt, to encourage native dialects.[2]

In material culture the Romanization advanced quickly. One uniform fashion spread from the Mediterranean throughout central and western Europe, driving out native art and substituting a conventionalized copy of Graeco-Roman or Italian art, which is characterized alike by technical finish and neatness, and by lack of originality and dependence on imitation. The result was inevitable. The whole external side of life was lived amidst Italian, or (as we may perhaps call it) Roman-provincial, furniture and environment. Take by way of example the development of the so-called 'Samian' ware. The original manufacture of this (so far as we are here concerned) was in Italy, chiefly at Arezzo. Early in the first century south Gaulish potters began to copy and compete with it ; before long, the products of the Arretine kilns had vanished even from the Italian market. Western Europe henceforward and even Italy were supplied with their 'best china' from provincial and mainly from Gaulish sources. The character of the ware supplied is significant. It was provincial, but it was in no sense unclassical. It drew many of its details from other sources than Arezzo, but it drew them all from Greece or Rome. Nothing either in the manner or in the matter of its decoration recalls native Gaul. Throughout, it is imitative and conventional, and, as often

[1] Even to the Celtic-speaking Treveri of the fourth century its sound must have been familiar. Cf. Ausonius, *Mosella*, p. 383, *Aemula te Latiae decorat facundia linguae*. It is the river that is addressed, but the context refers partly to Trier city.

[2] Mommsen (*Röm. Gesch.* v. 92) ascribes the final extinction of Celtic in northern Gaul to the influence of the Church. But the Church was not itself averse to native dialects ; its insistence on Latin in the west may be due rather to the previous diffusion of that language. (I am glad to see that Cumont (*op. cit.* p. 108) agrees with me.)

happens in a conventional art, items are freely jumbled together which do not fit into any coherent story or sequence ; many Gaulish potters seem to have been mainly anxious to leave no undecorated spaces on their bowls. At its best, it is handsome enough, though its possibilities are limited by its brutal monochrome. But it reveals unmistakably the Roman character of the civilization to which it belongs.

This Romanization in material things means more than is always recognized. Some scholars, in particular (perhaps) philologists, write as if the external environment of daily life, the furniture and decorations and architecture of our houses, the buckles and brooches of our dress, bear no relation to our personal feelings, our political hatreds, our national consciousness. That may be true to-day of Asiatic or African who dons European clothes once or again for profit or for pleasure. It was not true of the Roman provincial. When he adopted, and adopted permanently, the use of things Roman, we may say of him, firstly, that he had become civilized enough to realize their value, and further, that he had ceased to bear any national hatred against them. Such hatred must have existed here and there ; Tacitus hints that it existed for a little while in Britain. But it was rare ; we can argue from the spread of Roman material civilization that provincial sentiment was growing Roman.

By what process the less material aspects of provincial life became Roman is less clear, because it was necessarily more subtle. We seem, however, to see, at least in western Europe, the same harmonious amalgamation of dominant Roman elements with native elements that have not been wholly absorbed. In the east, of course, town-life and local government and land-tenure were mainly Hellenistic ; Romanization here made little way. But in the west there were towns enough of Roman foundation and Roman character (p. 15), with yet an intersprinkling of native developments. In northern and western Gaul, for instance, Roman municipalities (strictly so called) were wanting. Nevertheless, towns sprang up here, some through Roman official encour-

agement and some of spontaneous growth. These towns
were a cross between Roman and Gallic. They were the
' chefs-lieux ' of native cantonal areas and their local government was native. But the titles of their magistrates were
borrowed from the Roman municipal terminology and their
government was assimilated to the Roman municipal pattern;
even their town-plans were in some cases ' chessboards ' of
the received Italian type.[1] We shall meet some such towns
in Britain. In other provinces, as in southern Spain, hardly
a trace occurs of anything outside the strict Roman system.

So again in the sphere of religion. The Roman Empire
was generally tolerant of not-Roman worships, save in the
cases of Druidism and Christianity. It was rewarded. In
the western provinces the natives welcomed the Graeco-
Italian pantheon, identified their own gods with one or
another of its members, or, in default of identification, continued their old cults under new Latin names such as *deae
matres*. Religion is seldom logical or uniform, and the pre-
cise value to be put on these identifications doubtless varied
with every case and perhaps with every worshipper. Sometimes we may think we can see the old gods living on behind
their Roman masks and indeed keeping their power into the
Middle Ages. More often, Roman and native coalesced, and
again the exact proportions of the mingling must have in-
finitely varied. Some of the native cults seem to have survived more vigorously in the consciousness of the worshippers
than the others ; the one thing in which they agree is that
the Roman and the native are not hostile. There was
nothing unnatural to the provincial in honouring a Mercury
who was decked out in wholly Roman attributes—wand
and winged cap and purse and the rest—but who was placed
beside a provincial companion whose attributes declare her
the Celtic goddess Rosmerta (p. 73). The French scholar
Boissier once wrote that the civilized world was never nearer
to a common creed than under the Empire. Had it been
realized, it would have been a very complex creed.

[1] See my *Ancient Town-planning*, p. 120 and Fig. 29.

It remains true, of course, that, till a language or a custom is wholly dead and gone, it can always revive under due conditions. The rustic poor of a country seldom affect the trend of its history. But they have a curious persistent force. Superstitions, sentiments, even language and the consciousness of nationality, linger dormant among them, till an upheaval comes, till buried seeds are thrown out on the surface and forgotten plants blossom once more. The world has seen many examples of such resurrection—not least in modern Europe. The Roman Empire offers us singularly few instances, but it would be untrue to say that there were none.

Romanization was, then, a complex process with complex issues. It does not mean simply that all the subjects of Rome became wholly and uniformly Roman. The world is not so monotonous as that. In it two tendencies were blended with ever-varying results. First, Romanization extinguished the difference between Roman and provincial through all parts of the Empire but the east, alike in speech, in material culture, in political feeling and religion. When the provincials called themselves Roman or when we call them Roman, the epithet is correct. Secondly, the process worked with different degrees of speed and success in different lands. It did not everywhere and at once destroy all traces of tribal or national sentiments or fashions. These remained, at least for a while and in certain regions, not in active opposition, but in latent persistence, capable of resurrection under proper conditions. In such a case the provincial had become a Roman, but he could still undergo an atavistic reversion to the ways of his forefathers.

CHAPTER II

PRELIMINARY REMARKS ON ROMAN BRITAIN

ONE western province seems to break the general rule. In Britain, as it is described by many English writers, Roman and Briton were as distinct as modern Englishman and Indian, and 'the departure of the Romans' in the early fifth century left the natives almost as Celtic as their coming had found them nearly four hundred years before. The adoption of this view may be set down, I think, to various reasons which have, in themselves, little to do with the subject. The older archaeologists, familiar with the wars narrated by Caesar and Tacitus, pictured the whole history of the island as consisting of such struggles. Later writers have been influenced by the analogies of English rule in India. Still more recently, the revival of Welsh national sentiment has inspired a hope, which has become a belief, that the Roman conquest was an episode, after which an unaltered Celticism resumed its interrupted supremacy. These considerations have, plainly, little value as history, and the view which is based on them seems to me in large part mistaken. As I have pointed out, it is not the view which is suggested by a consideration of the general character of the western provinces. Nor do I think that it is the view which best agrees with the evidence which we possess in respect of Britain. In the following paragraphs I wish to examine this evidence. I shall adopt an archaeological rather than a legal or a philological standpoint. The legal and philological arguments have often been put forward. But the legal arguments are almost wholly *a priori*, and they have led different scholars to very different conclusions. The philological arguments are no less beset with difficulties.

Both the facts and their significance are obscure, and the inquiry into them has hitherto yielded little beyond confident and yet contradictory assertions which are incapable of proof. The archaeological evidence, on the other hand, is definite and consistent. It illuminates, not only the material civilization, but also the language and to some extent even the institutions of Roman Britain, and supplies, though imperfectly, the facts which our legal and philological arguments do not yield.

I need not here insert a sketch of Roman Britain. But I may call attention to three of its features. In the first place, it is necessary to distinguish the two halves of the province, the northern and western uplands occupied only by troops, and the eastern and southern lowlands which contained nothing but civilian life (Fig. 1).[1] The two are marked off, not in law but in practical fact, almost as if one had been *domi* and the other *militiae*. We shall not find much trace of Romanization in the uplands. There neither towns existed nor villas. Northwards, no town or country-house has been found beyond the neighbourhood of Aldborough (Isurium), some fifteen miles north-west of York. Westwards, on the Welsh frontier, the most advanced towns were at Wroxeter (Viroconium), near Shrewsbury, and at Caerwent (Venta Silurum), near Chepstow, and the furthest country-houses two isolated dwellings at Llantwit Major, in Glamorgan, and Llanfrynach, near Brecon.[2] In the southwest the last country-house was near Lyme Regis, the last town at Exeter.[3] These are the limits of the fully Romanized

[1] For details see the Victoria County Histories of *Northamptonshire*, i. 159, and *Derbyshire*, i. 191. I may say here that much of the evidence for the following paragraphs is to be found in my articles on Romano-British remains printed in various volumes of this History. I am indebted to its publishers for leave to reproduce several illustrations from its pages. For others I refer my readers to the History itself.

[2] See my *Military Aspects of Roman Wales*, notes 60 and 82. There was apparently some sort of town life at Carmarthen.

[3] West of Exeter Roman remains are few and mostly later than A.D. 250. No town or country-house or farm or stretch of roadway has ever been found here. The list of discoveries consists of : one

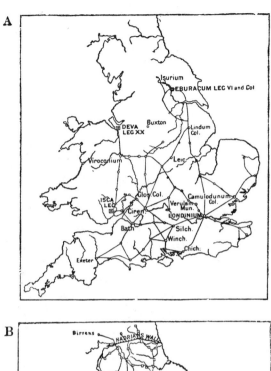

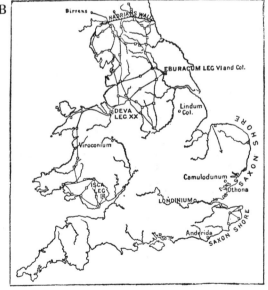

Fig. 1. (A) The Civil, (B) The Military Districts of Britain.

area. Outside of them, the population cannot have acquired much Roman character. Within these limits were towns and villages and country-houses and farms, a large population, and a developed and orderly life.

This sharp division between the military and civilian areas suggests that the garrison of Britain—the three legions at York, Chester, and Caerleon, and the ' auxiliaries ' scattered in *castella*, perhaps 30,000 or 35,000 men in all—had little influence on the civilization of Britain. At York, indeed, a town grew up outside the fortress (p. 57). But neither York nor Caerleon seem to have much affected the two country-towns near them, at Aldborough and Caerwent ; few other traces of civilization occur near either fortress, and Chester lay wholly beyond the pale. Possibly, as M. Cumont has observed,[1] the provisioning of the troops brought landowners and farmers into contact with the Roman system. But in general Britain must have, in this respect, differed much from northern Gaul and the Rhine frontier. There six legions and their ' auxiliaries ' watched 150 miles of frontier during the earlier Empire, and their influence on the Romanization of the border is very plain.

Secondly, the distribution of civilian life, even within these limits, was singularly uneven. It is not merely that some

early settlement on Plymouth harbour ; another near Bodmin, of small size, dating from the later first century ; a third, equally small and of uncertain date, on Padstow harbour ; some scanty vestiges of tin-mining, principally late ; two milestones (if milestones they be) of the early fourth century, at Tintagel church and at St. Hilary ; and some scattered hoards and isolated bits. Further, Mr. G. H. Wheeler (in a private letter) draws attention to a well-known charter dated A.D. 847 (*Cart. Saxon.* ii. 33 f.), which Mr. W. H. Stevenson (in his notes on Asser) has accepted as contemporary ; the description of the boundaries of the estate granted contains a reference to a ' stræte ', which, so early, might be Roman, and the estate itself appears not to have been in Dorsetshire, as the editor of the *Cart. Saxon.* suggests, but in Devon, at the neck of the peninsula which has Start Point at its S.E. extremity. Taken as a whole, the evidence indicates that portions of the country were inhabited, but that the inhabitants did not learn Roman ways, like those who lived east of the Exe. Even tin-mining was not pursued very actively till a comparatively late period, though the Bodmin settlement may be connected with tin-works close by.

[1] *Journal of Roman Studies*, ii. 113.

districts were the special homes of wealthier residents. We have also to conceive of some parts as densely peopled and of some as hardly inhabited. Portions of Kent, Sussex, Essex, and Somerset are set thick with ruins of country-houses and similar vestiges of Romano-British life. Other portions of the same counties, southern Kent, northern Sussex, south-eastern Essex, western Somerset, show few traces of any settled life. The midland plain, and in particular Warwickshire,[1] seems to have been the largest of these ' thin spots '. Here, among great woodlands and on damp and chilly clay, there dwelt not merely few civilized Roman-Britons, but few occupants at all.

Lastly, Romano-British life was on a small scale. It was, I think, normal in quality and indeed not very dissimilar from that of many parts of Gaul. But it was, in any case, defective in quantity. We find towns in Britain, as elsewhere, and farms and country-houses. But the towns are small and somewhat few, and the country-houses indicate comfort more often than wealth. So, too, the costlier objects of ordinary use, fine mosaics, precious glass, gold and silver ornaments, occur comparatively seldom,[2] and such as do occur, seem to be almost wholly imports. The great ' Lanx ', for instance, which was picked up on the bank of the Tyne near Corbridge, is not only the one eminently important piece of Roman silver found in the province ; it is also in all likelihood a product of the eastern Empire.[3]

---

[1] *Vict. Hist. of Warwickshire,* i. 228.

[2] See my remarks in Traill's *Social England* (illustrated edition, 1901), i. 141–61.

[3] *Journal of Roman Studies,* iv (1914), 1–12, with illustration. The very remarkable hoard of Roman silver discovered on Traprain Law in Haddingtonshire in May 1919 (*Proc. Soc. Ant. Scot.* liv. 102 ff.) has even less significance in this connexion. Apart from the fact that the ' find-spot ' had been well outside the boundaries of the province for more than two centuries before the approximate date of concealment (A.D. 400), it is not open to doubt that the treasure was loot from overseas.

In Roman Britain we have before us a civilization which, like a man whose constitution is sound rather than strong, might perish quickly from a violent shock.

A caution must be added. Geographically, Britain is an island tied closer than is always realized to the continent of Europe. The British lowlands are in the east and south ; right over against them, across a narrow sea, are the lowlands of the continent ; the rivers of island and continent flow out opposite each other ; it is easy from either shore to reach the other coast and to pass up into the land behind it. In both pre-Roman and Roman times it was constantly done. Therefore the same Celtic races dwelt on both sides of the sea ; there was frequent intercourse and the same or nearly the same civilization spread over northern Gaul and Britain from the Rhine to the Atlantic. In the districts of military life this civilization was crossed by the beliefs and customs and fashions of the soldiers ; elsewhere we deal with a Romano-Celtic—originally Celtic—civilization which requires to be studied more or less as a whole. It is useless to examine Roman Britain or Roman Gaul or even much of Roman Germany without constant reference to this whole, and much good work attempted by modern French or German or English archaeologists has failed to yield its proper fruit from neglect of this fact.

CHAPTER III

ROMANIZATION IN LANGUAGE

WE may now proceed to survey the actual remains. They may seem scanty, but they deserve examination.

First, in respect of language. Even before the Claudian conquest of A. D. 43, British princes had begun to inscribe their coins with Latin words. These legends are not merely blind and unintelligent copies, like the imitations of Roman legends on the early English *sceattas*. The word most often used, REX, is strange to the Roman coinage, and must have been employed with a real sense of its meaning. After A. D. 43, Latin advanced rapidly. No Celtic inscription has been detected, I believe, on any monument of the Roman period in Britain, neither cut on stone nor scratched on tile or potsherd, and this fact is the more noteworthy because Celtic inscriptions are not unknown in Gaul (see p. 31). On the other hand, Roman inscriptions occur freely in Britain. They are less common than in many other provinces, and they abound most in the northern military region. But they appear also in towns and country-houses of the low-lands, and some of the instances are significant.

The town site which we can best examine for our present purpose is Calleva Atrebatum (Silchester), ten miles south of Reading, which has been completely excavated within the circuit of its walls. It was a small town in a stoneless country; it can never have had many lapidary inscriptions, and such as there were must have been eagerly sought by later builders. Nevertheless, a few fairly perfect inscriptions on stone and many fragments have been found here and prove that the public language of the town was Latin.[1]

---

[1] For these and for the following *graffiti* see my accounts in the *Vict. Hist. of Hampshire*, i. 275, 282, and *Eph. Epigr.* ix. 984-8 and 1292-4 ; for the Clementinus tile see also *Archaeologia*, lviii. 30.

The speech of ordinary conversation is equally well attested by smaller inscribed objects, and the evidence is remarkable, since it plainly refers to the lower class of Callevans. When a weary brickmaker scrawls SATIS (enough) with his finger on a tile, or some prouder spirit writes FECIT TVBVL(*um*) CLEMENTINVS (Clementinus made this box-tile); when a bit of Samian is marked FVR (thief), presumably as a warning from the servants of one house to those of the next, or a brick shows the word PVELLAM, part of an amatory sentence otherwise lost, or another brick gives a Roman date, the ' sixth day before the Calends of October ', we may be sure

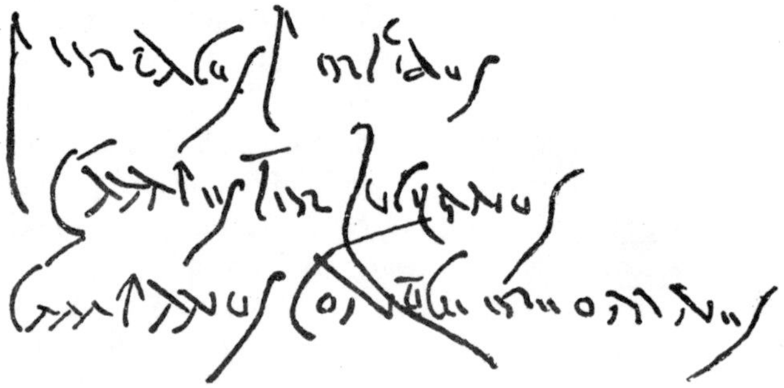

FIG. 5. GRAFFITO ON A TILE FOUND AT SILCHESTER (p. 30). *Pertacus perfidus | Campester Lucilianus | Campanus, conticuere omnes.*

that the lower classes of Calleva used Latin alike at their work and in their more frivolous moments (Figs. 2, 3, 4). When we find a tile scratched over with cursive lettering— possibly part of a writing lesson—which ends with a tag from the Aeneid, we recognize that not even Vergil was out of place here (Fig. 5).[1] The examples are so numerous and remarkable that they admit of no other interpretation.[2]

---

[1] Sir E. M. Thompson, *Greek and Latin Palaeography* (1894), p. 211, first suggested this explanation ; *Eph. Epigr.* ix. 1293.

[2] I have not, of course, quoted all. To call them—as did a kindly Belgian critic of this paper in its first published form—' un nombre de faits trop peu considérable ' is really to misstate the case.

Fig. 2. . . . *puellam*.

Fig. 3. *Fecit tubul(um) Clementinus.*

Fig. 4. *vi k(alendas) Octo[bres.* . . .

Figs. 2–4. Graffiti on Tiles from Silchester. (See p. 30.)

Griffith. certify that
the population spoke latin

I have heard this conclusion doubted on the ground that a bricklayer or domestic servant in a province of the Roman Empire would not have known how to read and write. The doubt rests on a misconception of the Empire. It is, indeed, akin to the surprise which tourists often exhibit when confronted with Roman remains in an excavation or a museum—a surprise that ' the Romans ' had boots, or beds, or waterpipes, or fireplaces, or roofs over their heads. There are, in truth, abundant evidences that the labouring man in Roman days knew how to read and write at need, and there is reason to believe that in the lands ruled by Rome education was better under the Empire than at any time since its fall till the nineteenth century.

It has, indeed, been suggested by doubters, that these *graffiti* were written by immigrant Italians, working as labourers or servants in Calleva. The suggestion does not seem probable. Italians certainly emigrated to the provinces in considerable numbers, just as Italians emigrate to-day. But we have seen above (p. 16) that the emigrants of the Imperial age were not labourers, as they are to-day. They were traders, dealers in land, money-lenders, or other ' well-to-do ' persons. The labourers and the servants of Calleva must be sought among the native population, and the *graffiti* testify that this population wrote Latin.

It is a further question whether, besides writing Latin, the Callevan servants and workmen may not also have spoken Celtic. Here direct evidence fails. In the nature of things, we cannot hope for proof of the negative proposition that Celtic was not spoken in Silchester. But all probabilities suggest that it was, at any rate, spoken very little. In the twenty years' excavation of the town, no Celtic inscription has emerged. Instead, we have proof that its lower classes wrote Latin for all sorts of purposes. Had they known Celtic well, it is hardly credible that they should not have sometimes written in that language, as the Gauls did across the Channel. In Gaul, potters of Roman date could scrawl their names and records, *Sacrillos avot*, ' Sacrillus potter ',

Valens avoti, ' Valens potter ', on a mould.[1] No such scrawl
has ever been found in Silchester or indeed in Britain.   In
Gaul, men with Roman names, Martialis and the like, could
set up inscriptions couched wholly or almost wholly in Celtic.
No such inscriptions occur in Britain.   The Gauls, again,
could invent a special letter Đ to denote a special Celtic
sound and keep it in Roman times.   No such letter was
used in Roman Britain, though it appears on earlier
British coins.   This total absence of written Celtic cannot
be a mere accident.

No other Romano-British town has been excavated so
fully or so scientifically as Silchester.   None, therefore, has
yielded so much evidence.   But we have no reason to con-
sider Silchester exceptional.   Such scraps as we possess
from other towns point to similar Romanization elsewhere.
Fvr, for instance, recurs on a potsherd from the Romano-
British country town at Dorchester in Dorset.   London
has yielded a tile on which, before it was baked hard, some
one scratched in unconventional Latin the remark, 'Austalis
goes off on his own daily for a fortnight.'   Austalis—that
is, Augustalis—was plainly a workman ; so was his critic,
and their fellow-workmen could presumably read and appre-
ciate the criticism.[2]   Leicester, too, supplies a tile scratched
Primus fecit x, ' Primus has made ten tiles.'[3]

The rural country-houses and farms, mostly ill-explored
and ill-recorded, furnish much scantier evidence than a carefully excavated town.   Yet they are not without their
Roman inscriptions cut on stone, for the most part dedications or tombstones, which prove that at least the owners
or occupiers of the houses claimed to know Latin.   Of the
more cogent *graffiti* on tiles or potsherds, examples are rare.

---

[1] *Avot* or *avotis* seems to be a Gaulish term for ' potter '.   One
example, *Sacrillos avot form.,* suggests a bilingual sentence such as we
find in some Cornish documents of the period when Cornish was
definitely giving way to English.

[2] *Austalis dibus* (i.e. *diebus*) *xiii vagatur sib(i) cotidim.*   See my
notes in *Eph. Epigr.* vii. 1141 and *Journal of Roman Studies,* i. 168,
plate xxvi.

[3] See *Eph. Epigr.* vii. 1143, and *Archaeol. Journ.* lxxv. 27.

FIG. 7. INSCRIBED TILE FROM PLAXTOL, KENT.

The top of the tile shows traces of the line *parietalem* and most of the line *Cabriabanu* ;
the lower part shows the former in full and the traces of the latter. The third line
(... *icavit*) has here, as on all the fragments, failed to come out clearly. (P. 33.)

FIG. 8. FRAGMENT OF INSCRIBED JAR FROM ICKLETON, CAMBS. (P. 33.)

But the man who made the tiles for a house at Plaxtol in Kent thought it worth while to cover them with Roman lettering; apparently he incised the legend in three lines on a wooden cylinder and rolled it over the tiles while soft, thus producing a recurrent inscription, 'Cabriabanus (or Cabriabantus) made this wall-tile' which served as a sort

Fig. 6. Reconstruction of the Plaxtol Inscription from Various Fragments.

The legend is, line 1 PARIETALEM, 2 CABRIABANVs (or NTVs), 3 . . . ICAVIT; line 1 is topsy-turvy to the rest. In Fig. 6 CAB in 2 and IT in 3 are repeated twice, to show the recurrence of the lettering.

of decoration (Figs. 6 and 7).[1] Again, two pieces of a blackish urn found long ago in the Roman farm at Ickleton, in south-east Cambridgeshire, bear a *graffito* which may be completed *ex ha]c amici bibun[t*, 'from this jar friends drink' (Fig. 8).[2] Yet once more, a Roman site near Easton Grey, in north Wiltshire, has yielded a little bas-relief carved (as it seems) in local stone with the figures of a goddess and three worshippers; the mason has roughly signed it, *Civilis fecit*, 'Civilis made me.'

[1] *Proc. Soc. Antiq. Lond.* xxiii. 108 and *Eph.* ix. 1290. The third line may possibly have read FAVRIGAVIT, a form intermediate between *fabricavit* and the French *forgeat*.

[2] C.I.L. vii. 1335. 7. Now at Audley End, where I have seen it. Too little remains of the jar to fix its date; it does not suggest the later Empire.

The general result is clear.   Latin was employed freely in the towns of Britain, not only on serious occasions or by the upper classes, but by servants and workpeople for the most accidental purposes.   It was also used, at least by the upper classes, in the country.   Plainly there did not exist in the towns that linguistic gulf between upper class and lower class which can be seen to-day in many cities of eastern Europe, where the employers speak one language and the employed another.   On the other hand, it is possible that a different division existed, one which is perhaps in general rarer, but which can, or could, be paralleled in some Slavonic districts of what was formerly Austria-Hungary.   That is, the townsfolk of all ranks and the upper class in the country may have spoken Latin, while the peasantry may have used Celtic.   No actual evidence has been discovered to prove this. It is not, however, in itself an improbable linguistic division of Roman Britain, even though the province did not contain any such racial differences as those of German, Pole, Ruthene and Rouman which lend so much interest to towns like Czernowitz.

It remains to cite the literary evidence, distinct if not abundant, as to the use of Latin in Britain.   Agricola, as is well known, encouraged it, with the result (says Tacitus) that the Britons, who had hitherto hated and refused the foreign tongue, became eager to speak it fluently.   About the same time, as Plutarch mentions in his tract on the cessation of oracles, one Demetrius of Tarsus, a 'grammarian', was teaching in Britain (A.D. 80), and his teaching is recorded as nothing out of the ordinary course.[1]   Rather later, in A.D. 96, Martial boasts that he was read in Britain, and about A.D. 120 Juvenal alludes casually to British lawyers taught by Gaulish schoolmasters.   It is plain that by the second century Latin must have been spreading widely in the province.   We need not feel puzzled about the way in which the Callevan workman of perhaps the third or fourth century learnt his Latin.

---

[1] See *Eph. Epigr.* ix. 560 and Dessau, *Hermes*, xlvi. 156.

At this point we might wish to introduce the arguments deducible from philology. We might ask whether the phonetics or the vocabulary of the later Celtic and the English languages reveal any traces of the influence of Latin, as a spoken tongue, or give negative testimony to its absence. Unfortunately, the inquiry seems almost hopeless. The facts are obscure and open to dispute, and the conclusions to be drawn from them are quite uncertain. Dogmatic assertions are common. Trustworthy results are correspondingly scarce. One instance may be cited in illustration. It has been argued that the name ' Kent ' is derived from the Celtic ' Cantion ', and not from the Latin ' Cantium ', because, according to the rules of Vulgar Latin, ' Cantium ' would have been pronounced ' Cantsium ' in the fifth century, when the Saxons may be supposed to have learnt the name. That is, Celtic was spoken in Kent about 450. Yet it is doubtful whether Latin ' ti ' had really come to be pronounced ' tsi ' in Britain so early as A.D. 450.[1] And it is plainly possible that the Saxons may have learnt the name long years before the reputed date of Hengist and Horsa. The Kentish coast was armed against them and the organization of the 'Saxon Shore' established as early as about A.D. 300. Their knowledge of the place-name may be at least as old. No other difficulty seems to hinder the derivation of ' Kent ' from the form ' Cantium ', and the argument based on the name thus collapses. It would be impossible here to go through the list of cases which have been supposed to be parallel in their origin to ' Kent ', nor should I, with a scanty knowledge of the subject, be justified in such an attempt. I have selected this example because it has lately been emphasized by an eminent writer.[2]

[1] It is noticeable that the Romano-British river-name ' Derventio ' was taken over by the English as ' Derwente ', later ' Deorwente ', without any trace of the vulgar-Latin palatalization to ' tsi '. I am indebted to Mr. W. H. Stevenson for help in relation to these philological points.

[2] Vinogradoff, *Growth of the Manor*, p. 102.

CHAPTER IV

ROMANIZATION IN MATERIAL CIVILIZATION

FROM language we pass to material civilization. Here is a far wider field of evidence, provided by buildings, private or public, their equipment and furniture, and the arts and small artistic or decorative objects. On the whole this evidence is clear and consistent. The material civilization of the province, the external fabric of its life, was Roman, in Britain as elsewhere in the west. Native elements succumbed to the conquering foreign influence.

I. In regard to public buildings this is natural enough. Before the Claudian conquest the Britons can hardly have possessed large structures in stone, and the provision of them necessarily came with the Romans. The *fora*, basilicas, and public baths of the towns, such as have been discovered at Silchester, Caerwent and elsewhere, follow Roman models and resemble similar buildings in other provinces. The streets of the towns seem also to have been laid out on the 'chessboard' system of town-planning proper to Roman municipalities of the Empire; to this point I shall return in a later chapter (p. 64). The temples, however, both in town and country, show as a rule something more of a local pattern. They consist generally of a small square or nearly square *cella* or shrine, with a roofed portico or colonnade running round all its four sides, and an entrance usually from the east (Fig. 9); the building often stands in a large open irregular enclosure. This type of temple occurs at Silchester and Caerwent and on many rural sites; it occurs also in northern Gaul and as far east as the Rhine. It differs from the ordinary classical type, and is taken by good authorities to be of Celtic origin ; it may, however, be a variation from the classical type or even an amalgamation of classical and native.[1]

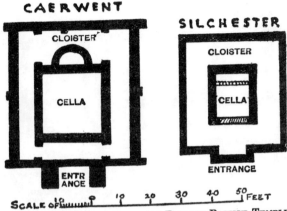

FIG. 9. TWO GROUND-PLANS OF ROMANO-BRITISH TEMPLES.

II. The private houses, by which I mean those built for civilized occupants, present more complicated features. Like dwelling-houses all the world over, they exhibit many varieties.[2] But we can distinguish two main types, called by English writers the Corridor and the Courtyard types. In the corridor house the front was formed by a narrow hall or corridor, which usually terminated at one or both ends

[1] For Gaulish instances of these temples, see Léon de Vesly, *Les Fana de la région Normande* (Rouen, 1909) ; for Germany, *Bonner Jahrbücher*, 1876, p. 57, Hettner, *Drei Tempelbezirke im Trevirerlande* (Trier, 1901) and *Trierer Jahresberichte*, iii. 49–66 ; they occur as far south as the Auvergne. The English writers who have published accounts of these structures have tended to ignore their special character. The temple unearthed at Wroxeter in 1913 seems to have belonged to the classical type, like that at Lydney. And the same is true of the remarkable remains under the Norman Castle at Colchester, to which attention has lately been drawn and which are believed by those who have examined them to represent the substructure of a temple. Their proportions are said to tally exactly, and their actual dimensions very closely, with those of the Maison Carrée at Nîmes : see *Journal of Roman Studies*, ix. 146 f.

[2] In the Victoria History (*Hants, Northants, Shropshire, Somerset*) I have given some twenty-five plans, which make up a fairly representative series.

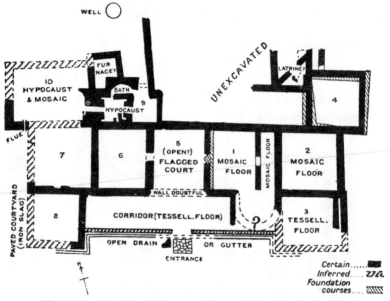

FIG. 10A. CORRIDOR HOUSE AT BRISLINGTON, NEAR BRISTOL
(see p. 39) (for scale see Fig. 10B).

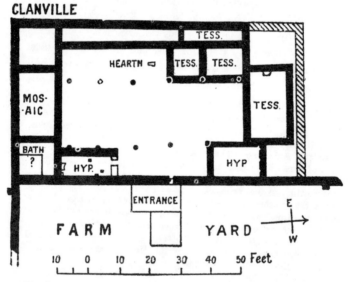

FIG. 10B. HOUSE AT CLANVILLE, NEAR ANDOVER, HANTS.
(See p. 39.)

[HYP. = hypocaust; TESS. = plain tessellated floor.]

in a largish room projecting slightly in wing-fashion. Houses of this class were common in Roman Britain. Many were small and poor; in the Frilford farmsteading, shown in Fig. 11, the wing-room must have been almost the only comfortable apartment, and much of the house may have

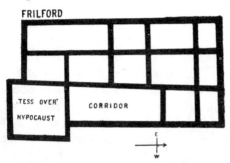

FIG. 11. PLAN OF FARMHOUSE AT FRILFORD, BERKS. (*From plan by Sir A. J. Evans*). The scale is the same as that of Figs. 10A and B on p. 38.

served farm purposes. Others were more luxurious; corridor houses at Brading, and at Brislington, near Bristol (Fig. 10A), seem to have been the homes of wealthy owners.

In the second or Courtyard type, the rooms were ranged along corridors which enclosed three—less commonly two or four—sides of a spacious squarish-yard (Fig. 12). Such houses were naturally extensive, and many were clearly the residences of rich men. In one form or another they are not much less common than the corridor houses. But the two types run into one another, and it is sometimes hard to decide whether a house consisting of a centre and two short wings should be called a corridor house with wing-rooms overgrown or a courtyard house with stunted flanks.

A third and far rarer type[1] shows a narrow oblong

[1] This type is sometimes thought to have been purely British. But what is perhaps a parallel, from Kastell Larga near Friesen (Kreis Altkirch), is described in *Westd. Zeitschrift*, xxvi. 273 ff., with plan (Taf. 2). The writer compares houses at Bachenau, Aulfingen, and Siblingen. The Larga house was built in the second century, and apparently surrounded by a defensive wall in the fourth. See also F. Oelmann in *Germania*, 1921, pp. 64 ff.

building, generally furnished with living-rooms at each end, while a double row of columns runs down its central portion. Its ground-plan strangely resembles that of a great columned barn, but it is possible that the middle space between the columns was really open to the sky and that the columns supported the roofs of sheds or colonnades. Some houses of this type possessed good mosaics and comfortable fittings ; more often they were subsidiary to better houses of the courtyard or corridor type, standing close by them and providing perhaps quarters for servants and the like. Fig. 10B shows one of these houses in which parts of the original sheds or colonnades have been built up into rooms.[1]

Corridor and courtyard houses occur freely both in town and in country ; the third type has been as yet detected only in the country. It is noteworthy that no special type of town-house occurs. Apart from a few shops—simple structures with shop in front and living-rooms or stores behind—the dwellings of Silchester (Fig. 13) and Caerwent are much the same as those of the countryside, and what is known of other towns, of Wroxeter or Aldborough, tells the same tale. Excavation may some day show us town-houses somewhere, but we have enough evidence already to conclude that the distinction between town-houses and country-houses was substantially unrepresented in Roman Britain. Here, however, we touch on a feature of Romano-British town-life which belongs rather to Chapter VI.

Britain is not peculiar in its two main types of houses. Like the temples described above (p. 36), courtyard and corridor houses recur in very similar forms in northern Gaul. From the seacoast to the Rhine they are indeed the dominant types of houses.[2] At present they are attested only as country-houses, but that is perhaps because no complete

[1] *Vict. Hist. Hants*, i. 302, 316 ; *Archaeol. Journ.* lxvi. 35.
[2] Some plans of north Gaulish and German country-houses and farms are given by de Caumont, *Abécédaire* (ed. 2, 1870), pp. 379 foll., and Kropatschek, *VI. Bericht der röm.-germ. Kommission*, 1910–11, pp. 57–73. For others see the *Annales* of the Namur Archaeological Society and similar journals.

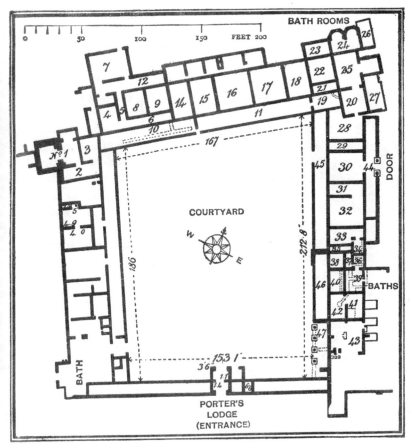

FIG. 12. COURTYARD HOUSE AT NORTHLEIGH, OXFORDSHIRE, AS
EXCAVATED IN 1815–16. Room 1, chief mosaic with hypocaust;
rooms 8–18, mosaic floors; rooms 21–7 and 38–43, baths, &c.; the
west wing had poorer rooms, perhaps for servants. Recent excavations show that this plan represents the house in its third and latest
stage; in the corridor (10) a part of the earlier house-front is shown
by dotted lines. The pottery found in the recent excavations suggests
that the first house on this spot was built not later than the early
second century. The place remained inhabited till the end of the Roman
period (c. 400 A.D.).

town-house has yet been uncovered in any Roman town of this region. The general likeness of Roman Britain to northern Gaul suggests that Amiens, Reims, Metz,[1] did not in this respect differ very greatly from Silchester.

The origin of these two northern types has been much discussed. English writers tend to think them Celtic, since they occur in Celtic lands ; they also see in the corridor an element common to both types, and suggest that the courtyard type grew out of the corridor type by gradually pushing forward its wing-rooms and continuing the corridor in front of them. Foreign writers more often derive them from types of houses used in Italy and the Greek east. Probably the material does not yet exist for a full settlement of the problem ; for one thing, we know too little of the rural dwellings of Italy, large or small. It is clear, however, that the Italian houses most familiar to us, the town-houses of Rome and Pompeii, bear no likeness to the northern houses. Their central feature is an *atrium*, and there is not an *atrium* to be found in any house in Roman Britain.

Probably the courtyard house has more connexion with the south than the corridor house. The town-houses of the Greek east and the kindred houses of Timgad in Africa, of Pola and Doclea in Adriatic lands—houses that are built round a small columned court or peristyle—offer faint parallels to our courtyard houses. Indeed, one or two houses at Silchester and Caerwent actually have such small courts.[2] More definite parallels, again to the courtyard type, can be found in other houses, mostly country-houses, of the same Greek type, which were built round large peristyles comparable in size to the spacious British and Gaulish

[1] Nor perhaps even Trier : a half-explored town-house at Trier is not at all Pompeian (*Bonner Jahrb.* ciii. 236).

[2] Silchester, *insula* xiv. 1 (*Archaeologia*, lv. 221) ; Caerwent, house 3 (*Arch.* lvii, plate 40). A few Pompeian houses have no *atrium* and belong to this type ; for instance, *ins.* v. 5 and vi. 15. Similarly, parallels may be drawn between certain Pompeian wall-paintings of houses and certain large houses in Germany, as at Nennig, Rouhling, Wittlich (see Rostowzew, *Archäol. Jahrbuch*, 1904, p. 103). But such houses are rare in Germany and unknown in Britain.

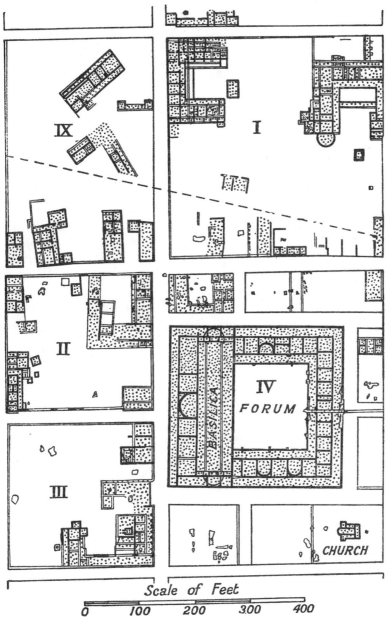

FIG. 13. PART OF SILCHESTER. Showing some private houses and shops, the Forum, and the Christian Church. (*From the plan by Sir W. Hope, issued by the Society of Antiquaries.*)

yards.[1] Perhaps we may conclude that our courtyard house owed much of its development to this originally Greek type. And if the peristyle house excavated in 1882 at Bibracte (Mont Beuvray), in mid-France, be of pre-Roman date, as Déchelette thought—and the evidence seems good— we may further guess that this type was spreading northwards as early as the age of Caesar.[2]

But the corridor house remains unfathered. To it Mediterranean lands offer no analogies. It has neither *atrium* nor peristyle, and the attempts of some scholars to detect pictures of it on two African mosaics are not convincing.[3] The most southern corridor house which I can quote was dug up years ago near Pau.[4] Perhaps, after all, we may credit it with a Celtic origin. That is the conclusion for which we should look on general grounds—that the larger and richer houses copied foreign patterns, while the smaller ones, like the Indian bungalow, tended to follow native lines. Here, as elsewhere, the Romanization of Britain combined native and Roman elements.

The internal fittings of these houses show the Roman supremacy more definitely. These fittings are wholly borrowed from Italian sources. If we cannot find in the Romano-British house either *atrium* or *impluvium, tablinum* or peristyle, such as we find in Italy, we have none the less the painted wall-plaster (Fig. 14) and mosaic floors, the hypocausts and bathrooms of Italy. The wall-paintings and mosaics may be poorer in Britain, the hypocausts more numerous ; the things themselves are those of the south.

---

[1] For instance, the large house of Fannius Sinistor near Pompeii ; a large house near Pola (Schwalb, *Römische Villa bei Pola*, Wien, 1902), an oil-farm on the same coast (Gnirs, *Jahrbuch für Altertumskunde*, ii. 134) ; a large house at Saint-Leu in Algeria (*Revue africaine*, 1894, p. 230), and the luxurious house in the town of Uthina (Oudna, in Tunis, see *Fondation Piot*, iii. 177).

[2] Bulliot, *Fouilles du Mont Beuvray* ; Déchelette, *Manuel*, ii. 953.

[3] Kropatschek (see p. 40, note) assumes that the corridor house was common in Italy. But that is pure assumption ; certainly the Bosco Reale farm is quite different. His arguments suffer also from his general neglect of all finds outside Germany.

[4] *Archaeol. Journ.* xxxvi. 17.

Fig. 14. Painted Pattern on Wall-plaster from Silchester.
Showing a conventional style based on classical models (p. 44).
(*Restoration by G. E. Fox, in Archaeologia.*)

No mosaic, I believe, has come to light in the whole of Roman Britain which represents any local subject or contains any unclassical feature. The usual ornamentation consists either of mythological scenes, such as Orpheus charming the animals,[1] or Apollo chasing Daphne, or Actaeon rent by his hounds, or of geometrical devices like the so-called Asiatic shields which are of classical origin.[2] Perhaps we may detect in Britain a special fondness for the cable or guilloche pattern, and we may conjecture that from Romano-British mosaics it passed in a modified form into later Celtic art. But the ornament itself, whether in single border or in many-stranded panels of plaitwork, occurs not rarely in Italy as well as in thoroughly Romanized lands like southern Spain and southern Gaul and Africa, and also in Greece and Asia Minor. It is a classical, not a British pattern.

III. Turn now to the dwellings of the peasant poor. These we know mainly in one corner of southern England, but within this limit we know them well. On the chalk downs of Wilts and north-east Dorset, Colt Hoare was busy a century ago, and in 1884–90 Pitt-Rivers dug three villages wholly up—at Woodcutts, Rotherley and Woodyates, a dozen miles south-west of Salisbury—and later workers have continued the search.[3] In plan these villages are not Roman;

---

[1] There is no reason to think the numerous Orpheus mosaics Christian. Christianity was not so ubiquitous as that. The scene, I imagine, was popular because it included various quaint animals.

[2] It has been suggested that these mosaics were laid by itinerant Italians. The idea is, of course, due to modern analogies. It does not seem impossible, since the work is in a sense that of an artist, and the pay might have been high enough to attract good decorators from the Continent. However, no evidence exists to prove this or even to make it probable. The mosaics of Roman Britain, with hardly an exception, are such as might easily be made in a province which could export skilled workmen to Gaul (p. 77). They have also the look of work imitated from patterns rather than of designs sketched by artists. It is most natural to suppose that, like the Gaulish Samian ware—which is imitative in much the same fashion,—they are local products.

[3] R. Colt Hoare, *Ancient Wiltshire* (1812–21); A. Pitt-Rivers, *Excavations in Cranborne Chase, &c.* (four large quartos, privately printed, 1887–98); M. E. Cunnington, *Wilts Archaeol. Magazine,*

their round mud-huts and pits, their strange ditches, their shapeless enclosures, date from days before or early in the Roman occupation. But Roman civilization soon reached and absorbed them. The ditches were filled up ; hypocausts, odd but unmistakable, wall-plaster painted in Roman fashion, roofing of Roman tiles, came into use ; the villagers learnt to eat and drink from Samian dishes and cups of glass, and even to keep their clothes in wooden chests of drawers ; some of them could read and write.[1] Meanwhile, they utterly forgot their Celtic fashions ; there is no sign of the Late Celtic art in any of Pitt-Rivers's multitudinous illustrations. To these men the Roman objects which they used were the ordinary environment of life ; they were no ' delicate exotic varnish ', as one eminent writer has called them.[2] Indeed, I cannot find in our Romano-British remains the contrast alleged by this writer ' between an exotic culture of a higher order and a vernacular culture of a primitive kind '. There were in Britain splendid houses and poor ones. But a continuous gradation of all sorts of buildings and all degrees of comfort connected them ; there is no discernible breach in the scale. Throughout, the dominant element is the Roman provincial fashion which is borrowed from Italy.

We find Roman influence even in the most secluded villages of the upland region. At Din Lligwy, on the northeast coast of Anglesea, excavation (Fig. 15) has uncovered the ruins of a village enclosure about three-quarters of an acre in extent, containing round and square huts or rooms, with walls of roughly coursed masonry and roofs of tile. Scattered up and down in it lay hundreds of fragments of

xxxvii. 42, xxxviii. 53 ; Heywood Sumner, *Excav. on Rockbourne Down* (London, 1914). Very similar results have been obtained in Berkshire : see D. Atkinson, *The Romano-British Site on Lowbury Hill* (Reading, 1916).

[1] Pitt-Rivers, iii. 3–6. So Colt Hoare, *Ancient Wilts, Roman Aera*, p. 127 : ' On some of the highest of our downs I have found stuccoed and painted walls, as well as hypocausts, introduced into the rude settlements of the Britons.'

[2] Vinogradoff, *Growth of the Manor*, p. 39.

Samian and other Roman or Romano-British pottery and a far smaller quantity of ruder pieces, a few bits of Roman glass, some Roman coins of the period A.D. 250–350, various iron nails and hooks, querns, bones, and so forth.[1] The place lies on the extreme edge of the British province and on an island where no signs of proper Roman occupation can

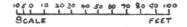

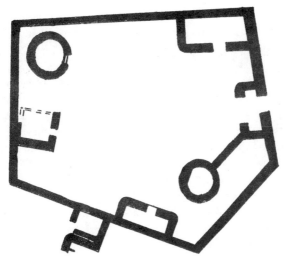

FIG. 15. NATIVE VILLAGE AT DIN LLIGWY, ANGLESEA.

be detected, while its ground-plan shows little mark of Roman influence. Yet the smaller objects and perhaps also the squareness of one or two rooms show that even here, in the later days of the Empire, the products of Roman civilization and the external fabric of Roman provincial life were present and almost predominant. The recent excavations on Traprain Law in Haddington teach precisely the same lesson.[2]

[1] E. Neil Baynes, *Arch. Cambrensis*, 1908, pp. 183–210.
[2] A. O. Curle, *Proc. Soc. Ant. Scot.* l, pp. 139 ff., and liv, pp. 99 ff.

CHAPTER V

ROMANIZATION IN ART

ART shows a rather different picture. Here the definite survivals of Celtic tradition are not perhaps more numerous but are certainly more tangible. There flourished in Britain before the Claudian conquest a vigorous native art, chiefly working in metal and enamel, and characterized by its love for spiral devices and its fantastic use of animal forms (Fig. 16). This art—La Tène or Late Celtic or whatever it be styled— was common to all the Celtic lands of Europe just before the Christian era, and its vestiges are particularly clear in Britain. When the Romans spread their dominion over the island, it almost wholly vanished. For that we are not to blame any evil influence of this particular Empire. All native arts, however beautiful, tend to disappear before the more even technique and the neater finish of town manufactures. The process is merely part of the honour which a coherent civilization enjoys in the eyes of country folk. Disraeli somewhere describes a Syrian lady preferring the polish of a western boot to the jewels of an eastern slipper. With a similar preference the British Celt abandoned his national art and adopted the Roman provincial fashion.

He did not abandon it wholly. Little local manufactures of small objects witness to sporadic survivals. Such, among pottery, are the New Forest stoneware with its curious leaf-ornament (Fig. 17), which was used a good deal in southern Britain,[1] and the better known and far more widely distributed Castor ware, made on the banks of the Nen some five miles west of Peterborough. We may briefly examine this latter instance.

---

[1] *Vict. Hist. Hants*, i. 326 ; *Archaeol. Journ.* xxx. 319. Much light has been thrown on the New Forest industry by the series of reports which Mr. Heywood Sumner has published at the Chiswick Press— *Ancient Earthworks of the New Forest* (1917), pp. 30 ff. ; *Descriptive Account of the Roman Pottery made at Ashley Rails* (1919) ; *Descriptive Account of Roman Pottery Sites at Linwood* (1921).

Fig. 16. Late Celtic Metal Work (⅓).

Boss of a shield, of perhaps the first century B.C., found in the Thames near Wandsworth, and now in the British Museum. See p. 48.

At Castor and Chesterton, on the north and south sides of the river, were two Romano-British settlements of comfortable houses, furnished in genuine Roman style.   Round them stretched extensive pottery works, which seem to have been active during the greater part of the Imperial period. The ware, or rather the most characteristic of the wares

Fig. 17.   Fragments of New Forest Pottery with Leaf Patterns.
(*From Archaeologia.*)   See p. 48.

made in these works, is generally called Castor (or sometimes Durobrivian) ware.   It was not, indeed, peculiar to the potters of the Nen valley.   There is evidence that, to some small extent at least, it was made elsewhere in Britain, and it must have been produced freely in northern Gaul, though none of its kilns has yet been identified there ; possibly it was produced there first and afterwards copied in Britain. But Castor is the only attested centre of its manufacture on a large scale, and the cups and jars from its potteries seem not only to be more abundant but also more varied in decoration and sometimes more directly inspired by native elements than the continental fabrics.[1]

Castor ware was decorated by the method often called ' barbotine ' ; the ornament was in relief and was laid on by hand in the form of a semi-liquid ' slip ' with the aid of a tube or other tool—just as in the later Roman Empire the ornament was laid on glass,[2] or as in our own day it is put on sugar-cakes. Every piece is, therefore, the individual product of a potter, not a mechanical cast from a mould. From this point of view it is noteworthy that the British Castor ware directly embodies the Celtic tradition. If it was copied from the Continent, the island potters either took over with it an element which has all but disappeared from the Gaulish work, or else they added that element. Castor ware is based, indeed, on classical patterns—foliated scrolls, hunting scenes, gladiatorial combats, even now and then a mythological representation. But it recasts these patterns in accordance with its own traditions and also with the vigour of a true art. Those fantastic animals with strange outstretched legs and back-turned heads and eager eyes ; those tiny scrolls scattered by way of background above and below them ; the rude beading which serves, not ineffectively, for ornament or for dividing line ; the suggestions of returning spirals ; the manifest delight of the artist in plant and animal forms—all these things are Celtic (Figs. 18, 19).

When we turn to the scenes in which man is prominent— a hunting picture in which (exceptionally) the huntsman

---

[1] Good illustrations of Continental Castor ware are given in *Sammlung Niessen*, Köln, 1911, plates 77, 78. For green-glazed specimens see *Bonn. Jahrb.* lxxiv. 150, plate vii, and lxxxiv. 117, plate iv. Continental manufacture, possibly near Cologne, seems to be proved by the amount of the ware found in the Low Countries, North France and Germany. Cumont (*Belgique romanisée*, p. 67) inclines to the view that all the Continental examples were imported from Britain. He argues, however, from their geographical distribution only, and takes no account of such evidence of origin as is adduced by Curle, *Roman Frontier Post*, p. 255 f. In Germany the production is said to have begun before A.D. 100 and to have ceased soon after A.D. 200. Its decoration is almost wholly confined to rather stereotyped animals, but the Colchester ' gladiators' urn ', mentioning the Thirtieth Legion (C. R. Smith, *Coll. Ant.* iv. 82 ; C.I.L. vii. 1335. 3), may be Rhenish manufacture.

[2] Kisa, *Glas im Altertume*, ii. 475.

FIG. 18. CASTOR WARE FOUND AT CASTOR NOW IN THE PETERBOROUGH MUSEUM. (P. 50.)

FIG. 19. HUNTING SCENES FROM CASTOR WARE (ARTIS, DUROBRIVAE). (P. 50.)

appears, or a chariot race, or a gladiatorial show, or Hesione
fettered naked to a rock and Hercules saving her from the
sea-monster (Fig. 20)[1]—we do not always find the same skill
and vigour. From of old the Celtic artist had been averse
to representations of the human form. When with an
initiative lacking in his continental rival—an initiative

FIG. 20. HERCULES RESCUING HESIONE. (*From a piece of Castor ware
found in Northamptonshire.* C. R. Smith, *Coll. Ant.*, vol. iv, Pl. XXIV.)

which it is fair to recognize—he added this to his repertory,
he passed beyond his proper bounds. Now and then he succeeded ; more often he failed ; his Hercules and Hesione
are not fantastic but grotesque. In taking in new Roman
elements, his Celtic art lost its power and approximated to
the conventionalism of Samian ware.[2]

Brooches tell much the same tale of predominant Roman
fashions not unmixed with Celtic survivals. Many of those
found in Britain are peculiarly British. One of the com-

---

[1] This and the corresponding scene of Perseus and Andromeda were
popular in Britain and Gaul. See (e.g.) a tombstone at Chester
(*Grosvenor Museum Catal.* No. 138), and others at Trier (Hettner,
Steindenkmäler zu Trier, p. 206) and Arlon (Wiltheim, *Luciliburgensia*,
plate 57) and Igel. Whether the scenes generally conveyed any
symbolical meaning in these lands, I should greatly doubt.

[2] For an account of Castor and Castor ware see *Vict. Hist. Northants*,
i. 166–78, 206–13.

monest of Romano-British ' fibulae ' (Fig. 21), commoner in
the north than in the south of the island, is not only directly
traceable to a Celtic ancestry, but is very rare outside Britain.[1]
The examples which have been found in northern Gaul and
Germany can almost be counted on the fingers of two hands ;
and when a specimen once turned up near Frankfurt, it
so startled the local archaeologists that they assigned it to

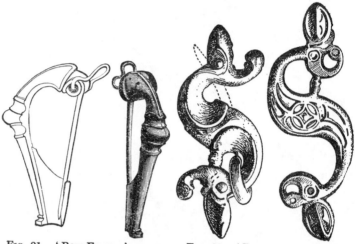

FIG. 21. ' BOW FIBULA ' FOUND
AT WOODEATON, OXON (¼).

FIG. 22. ' DRAGON-BROOCHES '
FOUND AT CORBRIDGE (¼). (P. 52.)

Africa. But the most striking example is supplied by the
enamelled ' dragon-brooches ' (Fig. 22). Both their designs
and their gorgeous colouring are Celtic in spirit ; they occur
not seldom in Britain ; from the Continent only four or five
instances are recorded.[2] Here certainly Roman Britain is more
Celtic than Gallia Belgica or the Rhine valley. Yet a complete
survey of the brooches used in Britain would show, especially
in the south, a dominant array of types which were equally
common here and on the Continent and belong to the
Roman provincial civilization. The ' Aucissa ' and ' knee '
and ' cross-bow ' varieties may serve as examples.

[1] For the origin of the type see Sir A. J. Evans, *Archaeologia*, lv. 182 ;
for additional illustrations and for the distribution, my note, *Arch.
Aeliana*, 1909, p. 400, and Curle, *Roman Frontier Post*, p. 321.

[2] I have given a list in *Arch. Aeliana*, 1909, p. 420 ; see also Curle,
Roman Frontier Post, p. 319, and R. A. Smith, *Proc. Soc. Antiq. Lond.*
xxii. 61. In all about twenty examples have been noted in Britain.

Fig. 23. The Corbridge Lion. (p. 53.)

Perhaps it is to this survival of the Celtic spirit in a Romanized Britain that we should ascribe two remarkable sculptures found at Bath and at Corbridge. The Spa at Bath (Aquae Sulis) contained a stately temple to Sul or Sulis Minerva, goddess of the hot springs. The pediment of this temple, partly preserved by a lucky accident and unearthed in 1790, was carved with a trophy of arms—in the centre a round wreathed shield upheld by two Victories, and below and on either side a helmet, a standard (?), a cuirass, besides other details now lost. It is a classical group, such as occurs on other Roman reliefs. But its treatment breaks clean away from the classical. The sculptor placed on the shield a Gorgon's head, as suits alike Minerva and a shield (see Frontispiece). But he gave to the Gorgon a beard and moustache, almost in the manner of a head of Fear, and he wrought its features with a fierce virile vigour that finds no kin in Greek or Roman art. I need not here discuss the reasons which may have led him to add male attributes to a female type. For our present purpose the important fact is that he could do it. Here is proof that, for once at least, the supremacy of the dominant conventional art of the Empire could be rudely broken down.[1]

Another example is supplied by the Corbridge Lion, found among the ruins of Corstopitum in Northumberland in 1907 (Fig. 23). It is a sculpture in the round showing a nearly life-sized lion standing above his prey. The scene is common in provincial Roman work, and not least in Gaul and Britain. Often it is connected with graves; sometimes (as perhaps here) it served for the ornament of a fountain. But if the scene is common, the execution of it is not. Technically, indeed, the piece is open to criticism. The lion is not the ordinary beast of nature. His face, the pose of his feet, the curl of his tail round his hind leg, are all untrue to life. The

---

[1] For the temple and pediment see *Vict. Hist. Somerset*, i. 229 foll., and references given there; I have discussed the artistic problem on p. 235 and *Journal of Roman Studies*, ii. 132. More recently, M. Adolphe Reinach suggested that the head embodies a definite Celtic idea (*Bull. du musée de Mulhouse*, xxxvii).

man who carved him knew perhaps more of dogs than
lions. But he fashioned a living animal. Fantastic and
even grotesque as it is, his work possesses a wholly unclassical
fierceness and vigour, and not a few observers have remarked
when seeing it that it recalls not the Roman world but the
Middle Ages.[1]

These exceptions to the ruling Roman provincial culture
are rare in Britain. But they are probably commoner here
than in the Celtic lands across the Channel. In northern
Gaul we meet no such vigorous semi-barbaric carving as the
Gorgon or the Lion. At Trier, Metz, Arlon, Sens, there are
notable sculptures, but they are consistently classical in
style and feeling, and the value of this fact is none the
less if (with some writers) we find special geographical
reasons for the occurrence of certain of these sculptures.[2]

Exceptions are always more interesting than rules—even
in grammar. But the exceptions pass and the rules remain.
The Castor ware and the Gorgon's head are exceptions. The
rule stands that the material civilization of Britain was pre-
dominantly Roman. Except the Gorgon, every worked or
sculptured stone at Bath follows the classical conventions.
Except the Castor and New Forest pottery, all the better
earthenware in use in Britain obeys the same law. The
kind that was most generally employed for all but the meaner
purposes, was not Castor but Samian.[3] This ware is charac-

---

[1] *Arch. Aeliana*, 1908, p. 205; *Journal of Roman Studies*, ii. 148.

[2] Michaelis, Loeschke and others assume an early intercourse between
the Mosel basin and eastern Europe, and thereby explain both a statue
in Pergamene style, which was found at Metz and appears to have been
carved there, and also the Neumagen sculptures. As all these pieces
were produced in Roman times, early intercourse seems an inadequate
cause. Moreover, Pergamene work, if rare in Italy, occurs in Aquitania
and Africa, and may have been popular in the provinces.

[3] I may protest against the attempts made from time to time to
dispossess the term ' Samian '. Nothing better has been proposed, and
it has the merit of perfect lucidity. Of the substitutes suggested,
' Pseudo-Arretine ' is clumsy, ' Terra Sigillata ' is at least as incorrect,
and ' Gaulish ' covers only part of the field (*Proc. Soc. Antiq. Lond.*
xxiii. 120).

teristic of Roman provincial art. As I have said, it is copied wholesale from Italian originals (p. 19). It is purely imitative and conventional; it reveals none of that delight in ornament, that spontaneousness in devising decoration and in working out artistic patterns which can clearly be traced in Late Celtic work. It is simply classical, in an inferior degree.

The contrast between this Romano-British civilization and the native art which preceded it can readily be seen if we compare for a moment a Celtic village and a Romano-British village. Examples of each have been carefully excavated in the south-west of England, hardly thirty miles apart. The Celtic village was close to Glastonbury in Somerset.[1] Of itself it was a small, poor place—just a group of pile-dwellings rising out of a marsh and dating from the two centuries immediately preceding the Christian era. Yet, poor as it was, its art is distinct. There one recognizes all that delight in decoration and that genuine artistic instinct which mark Late Celtic work, while technical details in the ornament (as, for example, the returning spiral) reveal their affinity with the same native fashion. On the other hand, no trace of classical workmanship or design intrudes. There has not been found anywhere in the village even a 'fibula' with a hinge instead of a spring, or of an Italian (as opposed to a Late Celtic) pattern.

Turn now to the Romano-British villages excavated by General Pitt-Rivers and already mentioned in these pages (p. 45). Here you may search in vain for vestiges of the native art or of that delight in artistic ornament which characterizes it. The ground-plans of the villages, the forms of the poor cottages, are native ; the art is Roman. Everywhere the monotonous Roman culture meets the eye. To pass from Glastonbury to Woodcutts is like passing from

[1] The Glastonbury village was excavated in and after 1892 at intervals ; a full account of the finds has been issued by Bulleid and Gray (*The Glastonbury Lake Village*, vol. i, 1911, with a preface by Dr. R. Munro; vol. ii, 1917). The finds themselves are mostly at Glastonbury.

some old timbered village of Kent or Sussex to the uniform streets of a modern city suburb. Life at Woodcutts had, no doubt, its barbaric side. One writer who has discussed it with a view to the present problem[1] comments on ' dwellings connected with pits used as storage rooms, refuse sinks, and burial places' and 'corpses crouching in un-Roman positions'. The first feature has its parallels in modern countries and was doubtless common in ancient Italy. The second would be more significant if such skeletons occupied all or even the majority of the graves in these villages. Neither feature really mars the broad result, that the material life was Roman. Perhaps the villagers knew little enough of Roman civilization in its higher aspects. Perhaps they did not speak Latin fluently or often. They may well have counted among the less Romanized of the southern Britons. Yet round them too clung the heavy inevitable atmosphere of the Roman material civilization.

[1] Vinogradoff, *Growth of the Manor*, p. 39. A parallel to the non-Roman burials found by General Pitt-Rivers may be found in the will of a Lingonian Gaul who died in the latter part of the first century (Dessau, 8379). He was a Roman citizen, and his will is drawn in strict Roman fashion. But its last clause orders the burning of all his hunting apparatus, spears and nets, &c., on his funeral pyre, and thus betrays the Gaulish habit.

That earlier native forms of burial were used in Roman Britain is shown by the remarkable burial mounds of the first and second centuries at Bartlow Hills in NW. Essex (*Archaeol.* xxv, xxvi, xxviii, xxix), Mersea Island (*Trans. Essex Arch. Soc.* xiii. 116), Rougham (*Vict. Hist. Suffolk*, i. 315), Gorsley Woods in East Kent (*Arch. Cantiana*, xv. 311), Thornborough in Bucks (remains at Audley End), and Youngsbury in Herts (*Archaeol.* lii. 287). They occur also in Belgium; see *Annales de la Soc. arch. de Namur*, xxiv. 50, and now Cumont *Belgique romanisée*, p. 88.

CHAPTER VI

ROMANIZATION IN TOWN-LIFE, LOCAL GOVERNMENT AND LAND-TENURE

I HAVE now dealt with the language and the material civilization of the province of Britain. I pass to a third and harder question, the administrative framework of local Romano-British life, the town-system and local government, and the land-tenure. Here we have to discuss especially the extent to which the Roman *coloniae* and *municipia* penetrated the province and the substitutes which arose instead of them, and the diffusion and influence of the Roman ' villa '. In respect to the towns and the local government, it has to be remembered that Roman, like Greek, towns were each the head of a dependent district, and therefore what we might now call the town and the county government more or less coincided.

I. First, the towns. Britain, we know, contained five municipalities of the privileged Italian type. The *colonia* of Camulodūnum (Colchester) and the *municipium* of Veru-lamium (St. Albans), both in the south-east of the island, were established soon after the Claudian conquest of A. D. 43. The *colonia* of Lindum (Lincoln) was probably founded in the early Flavian period (A.D. 70–80), when the Ninth Legion, hitherto at Lincoln, seems to have been pushed forward to York. The *colonia* at Glevum (Gloucester) arose in A.D. 96–98, as an inscription definitely attests. Lastly, the *colonia* at Eburacum (York) must have grown up during the second or the early third century, under the ramparts of the legionary fortress, though separated from it by the intervening river Ouse.[1] Each of these five towns had,

---

[1] The fortress was situated on the left or east bank of the Ouse ; the present cathedral stands wholly within its area. Parts of the

doubtless, its dependent territory, which may have been as large as an average English county, and each provided the local government for its territory.[1] That implies a definitely Roman form of local government for a considerable area—a larger area, certainly, than received such organization in northern Gaul. Yet it accounts, on a liberal estimate, for barely one-eighth of the civilized part of the province.

Throughout most of the rest of the British province, or rather of its civilized area, the local government was probably organized on the same cantonal system as obtained in northern Gaul (p. 21). According to this system, the local unit was the former territory of the independent tribe or canton, and the local magistrates were the chiefs or nobles of the tribe. That may appear at first sight to be a native system, wholly out of harmony with the Roman method of government by municipalities. Yet such was not its actual effect. The cantonal or tribal magistrates were classified and arranged just like the magistrates of a municipality. They even used the same titles. The cantonal *civitas* had its *duoviri* and quaestors and so forth, and its *ordo* or senate, precisely like any municipal *colonia* or *municipium*. So far from wearing a native aspect, this cantonal system became one of the influences which aided the Romanization of the country. It did not, indeed, involve, like the municipal system, the substitution of an Italian for a native institution. Instead, it permitted the complete remodelling of the native institution by the interpenetration of Italian influences.

Roman walls can still be traced, especially at the Multangular Tower. The municipality lay on the other bank of the Ouse, near the railway station, where mosaics indicate dwelling-houses. Its outline and plan are, however, unknown. Even its situation has not been generally recognized.

[1] If the evidence of milestones may be pressed, the territory of Eburacum extended southwards at least twenty miles to Castleford, and that of Lincoln at least fourteen miles to Littleborough (*Eph. Epigr.* vii. 1105 = ix. 1253, and vii. 1097). The general size of these municipal ' territoria ' is proved by Continental inscriptions. Numerous attempts have been made to detect ' centuriation ', or something like it, in Britain. But the evidence is very inadequate. See, however, *Engl. Hist. Review*, 1918, pp. 289 ff., and *Trans. Essex Arch. Soc.* xv (n.s.), 115 ff.

We can discern the cantonal system at several points in Britain.   But the British cantons were smaller and less wealthy than those of Gaul, and therefore they have not left their mark, either in monuments or in nomenclature, so

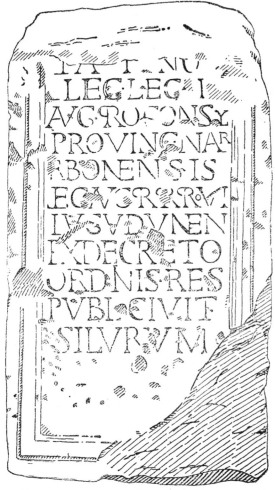

FIG. 24. INSCRIPTION FOUND AT CAERWENT MENTIONING A DECREE OF THE SENATE OF THE CANTON OF SILURES. SEE P. 60.

clearly as we might desire.   Many inscriptions record the working of the system in Gaul.   Many modern towns — Paris, Reims, Amiens, and thirty or forty others—derive

their present names from those of the ancient cantons, and
not from those of the ancient towns. Britain has hitherto
yielded only one such inscription (Fig. 24),[1] on a monument
erected at Caerwent (Venta Silurum) by the cantonal senate
of the Silures to some general of the Second Legion at Isca
Silurum, twelve miles off. Only one British town was called
in antiquity by a tribal name—and that is a doubtful
instance.[2] No single case occurs in which a modern town-
name is derived from the name of a British tribe.[3]

We have, however, some curious evidence from another
source. There is a late and obscure *Geography of the Roman
Empire* which was probably compiled at Ravenna somewhere
about A.D. 700, and which, as its author's name is lost, is
generally quoted as the work of ' Ravennas '. It consists
for the most part of lists of names, copied from sources far
earlier than the seventh century, and very carelessly copied.
In general it adds very few details. But in the case of
Britain it notes the municipal rank of three of the four
coloniae, and it further appends tribal names to nine or ten
town-names, which are thus distinguished from all other
British place-names. For example, we have Venta Belgarum
(Winchester), not Venta simply, and Corinium Dobunorum
(Cirencester), not Corinium simply. The towns thus specially
marked out are just those towns which are also declared by

---

[1] Found in 1903 : . . . *leg. leg.* [*i*]*i, Aug. proconsul*(*i*) *provinc. Narbonensis, leg. Aug. pr. pr. provi. Lugudunen*(*sis*) : *ex decreto ordinis
respubl*(*ica*) *civit*(*atis*) *Silurum.* It was probably set up to Claudius
Paulinus, early in the third century (*Athenaeum*, Sept. 26, 1903 ;
Archaeologia, lix. 120 ; *Eph. Epigr.* ix. 1012). Other inscriptions mention a *civis Cantius*, a *civitas Catuvellaunorum* and the like, but their
evidence is less distinct.

[2] *Icinos* in *Itin. Ant.* 474. 6 may be Venta Icenorum (*Victoria Hist.
of Norfolk*, i. 286, 300). In its Gaulish section the *Itin.* uses these
tribal town-names about as often as not.

[3] Canterbury may seem an exception. But its name comes ultimately
from the Early English form of Cantium, not from the Cantii. In the
south-west and in Wales, tribal names like Dumnonii (Devonshire),
Demetae, Ordovices, have lingered on in one form or another ; according to Prof. Rhŷs, Bernicia is derivable from Brigantes. But these
cases differ widely from the Gaulish instances.

actual remains to have been the chief country towns of Roman Britain.   This coincidence can hardly be chance. We may infer that the towns to which the Ravennas appends tribal names were the cantonal capitals of the districts of Roman Britain, and that a list of them, presumably mutilated and imperfect, has been preserved by some chance in this late corrupt compilation.[1]

In other words, the larger part of Roman Britain was divided up into districts corresponding to the territories of the Celtic tribes ; each has its capital, and presumably its magistrates and senate, as the above-mentioned inscription shows that the Silures had at Venta Silurum. We may suppose, indeed, that the district magistrates— the county council, as it would now be called—were also the magistrates of the country town.   The same cantonal system, then, existed here as in northern Gaul. Only, it was weaker in Britain.   It could not impose tribal names on the towns, and it went down easily when the Empire fell.   In northern Gaul, Nemetacum Atrebatum became Atrebatis and is now Arras.   In Britain, Calleva Atrebatum (Silchester) remained Calleva, so far as we know, till it perished altogether in the fifth century.

Municipalities and cantonal capitals furnish nearly all the known examples of Romano-British towns.   Two or three lesser places may have been secondary country-towns.[2] A spa, rather than a town proper, flourished at Bath, and attracted invalids from Britain and from northern Gaul. There is only one important addition to be made to our list.   Londinium sprang up in the earliest Roman period, on a spot marked out by trade advantages rather than by

---

[1] Ravennas (ed. Parthey and Pinder), pp. 425 foll. ; my Appendix to Mommsen's *Provinces of the Empire* (English trans., 1909), ii. 352. The places are those now known as : Exeter, Winchester, Caerwent, Cirencester, Silchester, Canterbury, Wroxeter, Leicester, Castor by Norwich, and probably Chichester : to these we may add from other sources Aldborough (Yorks) and Dorchester in Dorset.

[2] Rochester in Kent and Kenchester near Hereford are the only ones which merit mention here.

any noteworthy native settlement ; it quickly grew to be the largest and richest town in the province. But we never hear that it won municipal rank, and its civic constitution rested perhaps on a different basis. We know from Tacitus that it began as a gathering of traders round a convenient centre. We know also that the Roman provinces contained many such clubs or communities of Roman traders, ruling themselves on a quasi-municipal pattern (16, note 1). We may think that London was, at the outset, one of these communities, and that, while most of them grew into municipalities, it kept its original status unaltered. The Empire was as full of irregularities as the Greek accidence, and Roman opportunism loved to let well alone. London in the fourth century gained the title—honourable, if not rare—of Augusta, but remained in its quasi-municipal position.[1]

On paper this represents much Romanized town-life in Britain. Did the facts bear out the theory ? On the whole, we may say that they did. The Romano-British towns were of fair size. Silchester was by no means the biggest. Roman London, perhaps even Roman Cirencester, were larger than Roman Cologne or Bordeaux ; Verulam and others were not so far behind.[2] They possessed, too, the buildings proper to a Roman town—town-hall, market-place, public baths, ' chess-board ' street-plan, all of Roman fashion ; they had also shops and temples, and even here and there a hotel ; and it is to be noted that these were present not only 'in the municipalities, as it seems, but in

[1] Londinium is often credited with wonderful features—territory, pomerium, citadel, jurisdiction to a mile outside its gates, and so forth. No true view of it can be got, unless these be put aside.

[2] Within the walls, London was about 325 acres, Cirencester a little over 240, Cologne 240, Verulam 200, Silchester, Colchester and Leicester 110–100 acres. Comparisons, however, are difficult, even where the walled area is known, since sometimes (at London, Silchester, Trier, Cologne) the walls seem to have enclosed the town at near its largest, while elsewhere the walled area is but a fragment left after Teutonic invasion. For Bordeaux see Jullian, *Inscr. de Bordeaux*, ii. 588; at its zenith, he tells me, it perhaps covered 185 or 200 acres. For Cirencester see *Archaeologia*, lxix. 161 ff., and for Leicester *Archaeol. Journ.* lxxv. 1 ff.

the cantonal capitals as well. Whether and how far the municipalities had a stronger Roman colouring than the other towns, we do not know. But we can see that their Roman constitutions were realities; witness the tiles of Roman Gloucester, with their stamp RPG (*respublica Glevensium*) and their dating by municipal magistrates, the ' duoviri ' and ' quinquennales '.

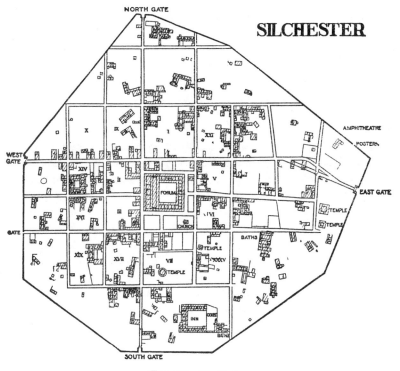

FIG. 25. (P. 64.)

Other details point somewhat the other way. We should have expected the British municipalities, like those of other provinces, to have helped in supplying the Roman army with legionaries and the Roman administration with officials. But, so far as present evidence goes, few Britons served in the legions and hardly any won official rank. Again, the plans of the towns known to us reveal a significant feature, which I have noted already (p. 40). The dwelling-houses in them are not town-houses, fitted to stand side by side and to form regular streets ; they are country-houses, such as neither did nor could combine in continuous rows; they are dotted about like cottages in a village (Figs. 12, 25). One recognizes that the town-planning of Silchester or Caerwent was introduced amid surroundings not fully urban and that it represents an attempt at municipalization for which the dwellers in Calleva and Venta were not ready. These men learnt town-life from Rome. They did not learn it in its highest form. Indeed, through all the rebuildings which the spade reveals in these towns, they clung till the end to their older rural fashion.[1]

Those who weigh these facts against one another will conclude, I think, that the Roman town-system of Britain was a real thing. It contained native as well as Roman elements ; here, as elsewhere, Romanization was a subtler and more complex process than mere absorption in Rome. The towns, too, were neither many nor very large ; here, as elsewhere, Romano-British life was on a small scale. But in one way or another and to a real amount, Britain shared in that expansion of town-life which formed a special achievement of the Roman Empire.

The towns and the districts connected with them occupied most of the British lowlands. Whatever was over, fell probably within the Imperial domains, which covered wide tracts in every province and were administered by local ' procurators ' of the Emperor. The lead-mining districts—Mendip in Somerset, the neighbourhood of Matlock in Derbyshire, the Shelve Hills south-west of Wroxeter, the Halkyn region in Flintshire, the moors of south-west Yorkshire—must have belonged to these Domains, and for the most part are actually attested by inscriptions on lead-pigs as Imperial property. Of other domain lands we meet what seems to be one early

[1] See further my *Ancient Town-planning*, pp. 127–35.

instance at Silchester in the reign of Nero [1]—perhaps the confiscated estates of some British prince or noble—and though we have no further direct evidence, the history of other provinces suggests that the area increased as the years went by. Yet it is likely that in Britain, as indeed in Gaul,[2] the domain lands were comparatively small in extent. Moreover, if we may trust analogies from Asia Minor, they probably contributed little to Romanization (p. 18).

II. It remains to say what little can be said as to the land-tenure of the province. Evidence on this point is unfortunately very scanty. We know next to nothing about either the size or the character of the estates which corresponded to the country-houses and farms of which remains survive. The ' villa ' system of demesne farms and serfs or *coloni*,[3] which obtained elsewhere, was doubtless familiar in Britain. Indeed, the Theodosian Code definitely refers to British *coloni*.[4] But whether it was the only rural system in Britain is beyond proof, and previous attempts to work out the problem have done little more than demonstrate the fact.[5] It is quite likely that here, as indeed in any

---

[1] Tile inscribed NERCLCÆA'GGꟼR, *Nero Claudius Caesar Augustus Germanicus* (*Eph. Epigr.* ix. 1267). It differs markedly from the ordinary Silchester tiles, and plainly belongs to a different period in the history of the site. Possibly the estate, or whatever it was, did not remain Imperial after Nero's fall ; compare Plutarch, *Galba*, 5. The Combe Down *principia* (C. vii. 62), which are not military, may supply another example, of about A.D. 210 (*Vict. Hist. Somerset*, i. 311 ; *Eph. Epigr.* ix. 516).

[2] Hirschfeld, *Klio*, ii. 307, 308. Much of the Gaulish domain land appears to date from confiscations in A.D. 197.

[3] The term ' villa ' is now generally used to denote Roman country-houses and farms, irrespective of their legal classification. The use is so firmly established, both in England and abroad, that it would be idle to attempt to alter it. Moreover, it was not unknown to Latin writers ; Ausonius, for instance, speaks (*Mosella*, l. 20) of *culmina villarum pendentibus edita ripis*, with which cf. Martial, iv. 64, 10. But for clearness I have in this paper employed the term ' villa ' only where I refer to the definite ' villa ' system.

[4] Cod. Theod. xi. 7. 2.

[5] For instance, Seebohm (*English Village Community*, pp. 254 foll.) connected the suffix ' ham ' with the Roman ' villa ' and apparently argued that the occurrence of the suffix indicated in general the former existence of a ' villa '. But his map, showing the percentage of local

E

province, other forms of estates and of land-tenure may have existed beside the ' villa '.[1] The one thing needed is evidence. Unfortunately, the sizes and relative positions of the country dwellings do not, of themselves, reveal much in this respect. In some Rhenish districts the houses are so uniform in plan and so evenly distributed as to suggest settlements of veteran soldiers. In Britain the evidence at present known points to a system which has grown up of itself but does not show the exact nature of that system.

In any case, the net result appears fairly certain. The bulk of British local government must have been carried on through Roman municipalities, through imperial estates, and still more through tribal *civitates* using a Romanized constitution. The bulk of the landed estates must have conformed in their legal aspects to the ' villas ' of other provinces. Whatever room there may be for the survival of native customs or institutions, we have no evidence that they survived, within the lowlands, either in great amount or in any form which conflicted with the general Romanized character of the country.

names ending in ' ham ' in various counties, disproves his view. For the distribution of the suffix ' ham ' and the frequency of Roman country-houses and farms do not coincide. In Norfolk, for instance, ' ham ' is common, but there is hardly a Roman country-house or farm in the county (*Victoria Hist. of Norfolk*, i. 294–8). Somerset, on the other hand, is crowded with Roman country-houses, and has hardly any ' hams '.

[1] Prof. Vinogradoff, *Growth of the Manor*, chap. ii, argues for the existence of Celtic land-tenures besides the Roman ' villa '. ' There was room (he suggests) for all sorts of conditions, from almost exact copies of Roman municipal corporations and Italian country-houses to tribal arrangements scarcely coloured by a thin sprinkling of imperial administration ' (p. 83). This is very probable. But I find no definite proof of it. If northern Gaul were better known, it might provide a decisive analogy. But the Gaulish evidence itself seems disputable.

CHAPTER VII

ROMANIZATION IN RELIGION

THE current religions of the modern world, monotheistic in character and eastern in origin, are exclusive; no man can be in any real sense Mahometan and Jew at once. The polytheisms of ancient Europe contained little to hinder combinations of creeds, and the Romans, being politic as well as polytheistic, encouraged the process. They had easily equated their own Italian gods with the gods of Greece; the provincials found it no harder to combine native provincial cults with the Graeco-Roman religion. The western half of the Empire thus became a blending-vat of worships, western and eastern and Roman. The ruling element was Roman. The native cults of western origin survived—at least on the surface—mainly as appendages of Roman deities; and even the far stronger eastern cults, Mithraism and the rest, took on somewhat of Roman dress. The outcome was too vague and ill-defined, and too various in different lands, to be called a Roman provincial religion. Rather, an equation of worships was established under Roman primacy, by which a man who changed his town or province, could change his gods as easily as he changed his washerwoman.

This happened also in Britain. The inscriptions and sculptures of our province show a mass of diverse cults which were united in their use of Latin and in their common Roman colouring. In detail, however, the military districts differ widely, as so often, from the districts of civilian life, in which the Romanized provincials dwelt. We may best group our survey into (1) cults which seem strictly Roman, (2) others which may be called Romano-Celtic, and (3)

others again which came to Britain from sources neither
Roman nor Celtic, but either Teutonic or Oriental.

I. Purely Roman dedications, such as an Italian might
have set up in Italy, are common enough in the military
area.   There we meet altars to Iuppiter Optimus Maximus
and other true gods of Rome, without any intermixture of
non-Roman religion.   But they are altogether rare in the
towns and country districts.   A few exceptions can be noted.
At Chichester in the middle of the first century a Roman-
izing native princelet set up a monument to Neptune and
Minerva.   In the midlands, near Stony Stratford, a man
with a Celtic name, Vassinus, made some sort of offering to
Jove and Vulcan.   A shrine in the Cotswolds contained a
figure of a god in full armour, carved in stone, with the
superscription *deo Romulo*, ' to the god Romulus.'   In a
few places we meet altars set up simply to Mars or Mercury or Aesculapius or Diana.   But the total list of these
plain Roman dedications is short.   Nor do we hear more
of the official worship of the Emperor.   Dedications to his
Divinity (*numina Augustorum*, &c.) are frequent in forts
and fortresses.   Elsewhere they are scanty.   In the *colonia*
of Camulodūnum was a temple for the official cult of Rome
and the Emperor ;[1] some years ago a boy fished out of a
Suffolk stream a bronze head which was probably pillaged
from it in the rising of Boudicca.   But we hear next to
nothing about the cult.   It not only had no religious value ; it
had not even the social importance which it enjoyed in Gaul.

II. Far commoner are Romano-Celtic and native dedications.[2]   Many of these are dedications to Roman gods with
Celtic epithets, to Mars Belatucader, Mars Cocidius, Mars
Corotiacus,—not to Mars simply.   It does not appear that
the varieties of Mars which were thus created wielded different
powers, or that you prayed to Mars Belatucader for one sort
of favour and to Mars Cocidius for another ; that doubtless
happened to some extent, but it does not seem to have been
common.   We may say rather that scattered, mostly local,

---

[1] Cf. p. 37, note 1.

[2] Anwyl's article in the *Cambridge Medieval History*, ii. 472–9, is,
I fear, unsatisfactory.

cults crystallized round Roman names. It was, however, only a few Roman gods—in Britain and in north Gaul Mars and Mercury—who attracted Celtic epithets to themselves at all freely. Apollo, Diana, Juno, Neptune, and the rest appear comparatively seldom or even never with them. On the other hand, a long series of dedications concern gods whose names are purely Celtic except for their Latin terminations. These are many. But they do not greatly differ from those just described; indeed, many Celtic deities appear now with, now without, the Roman prefix.

If we now proceed to classify the Celtic cults of which we meet remains in Britain, we must note first the absence of any hierarchy of great gods. Of Esus, Taranis and Teutates, sometimes styled the Celtic Trinity, no sign emerges.[1] Instead, a crowd of lesser deities reveals a primitive religion in much the same rudimentary state as were the religions of Greece and Rome before the Olympian gods had become acknowledged as supreme. Some bear names which seem descriptive of character. Such was Belatucader, ' good at war ', who was worshipped in the north and coupled with Mars. Such, too, Maponus, kin somehow to the Welsh ' Mabon ', a child, and habitually yoked with Apollo. Others belonged to natural features. Verbeia at Ilkley was patron saint of a stream still called Wharfe; the Northumberland Cocidius (often Mars Cocidius) may have begun as god of the Coquet. Others with less intelligible names were clearly connected with special spots; such were Ancasta at Bitterne (near Southampton), Coventina,

---

[1] Teutates occurs once, possibly twice, identified with Mars; the others are absent. A Chester altar (C.I.L. vii. 168) is said to read I O M TANARO, but the reading is uncertain; even if it be right, still Tanarus is not (as Mr. Holmes thinks, *Anct. Britain*, p. 279) the same as Taranis. Whether these three gods were really so important, is disputed; see Jullian, *Cambridge Medieval History*, ii. 464, (for) and S. Reinach, *Mythes et Cultes*, i. 205 (against). Mr. Holmes mistakes the position when he says that ' the devotee who composed his inscription to Toutates would not have wittingly ascribed to a mere local god the qualities of Mars '. That is just what they did, all over Britain and north Gaul.

whose sacred water bubbled up within the shadow of the Roman Wall, and Antenociticus, whose shrine now lies beneath a suburb of Newcastle. Sul or Sulis, thought to be by origin the Celtic female Sun and identified with Minerva, was goddess of the Bath waters. Nodens, kin to or bearing the same name as an Irish hero, Nuada of the Silver Hand, was worshipped in west Gloucestershire at Lydney.

These cults and others like them are British. Some Celtic dedications which occur in the province seem, on the other hand, to have been brought in from the Celtic mainland. Mars Leucetius (the lightning god), Mars Rigisamus (most royal), Mars Olludius, Apollo Grannus, belong across the Channel; Grannus, god of healing waters, had a home at Aachen. A Caerwent altar provides a signal example of how such import happened. It was set up by a quite unknown man, one Nonius Romanus, to Mars Lenus or Ocelus (*Marti Leno sive Ocelo*). Mars Lenus was a local saint in the Mosel valley; Mars Ocelus has been met again in Caerwent and also in the north. As the Celts of the Mosel were wont to emigrate freely, it is pretty plain that Nonius came thence to Caerwent; there he wished to honour the gods of his old and his new home, and equated the two in one phrase.[1] Another and much better known example of imported Celtic worship may be found in the Mother Goddesses, the *deae matres*. Every one who has looked into museums in the north of England or along the Rhine will be familiar with the curious reliefs which show the Three Mothers seated stiffly side by side, clothed in long robes and strange headdress and often holding on their laps round baskets of fruit. Their cult was common in north Italy and south-eastern Gaul, and on the middle and lower Rhine, and in Britain. But in Britain it is limited mainly to the army; its monuments occur, with comparatively few exceptions, within the military area, and the worshippers, so far as they state their professions, are nearly all soldiers.

---

[1] *Eph. Epigr.* ix. 1182 and my note. We may ascribe to another such immigrant the 'colonne au géant' at Cirencester (*Eph. Epigr.* ix. 997, and *Archaeologia*, lxix. 188 ff.).

Probably its birthplace was in the Celtic districts of northern
Italy and south-eastern Gaul, where the earliest dedications
have been found. There, during the early Empire, soldiers
were recruited in large numbers for service on the Rhine
and in Britain, and these soldiers took their native worship
with them. Only, from the Rhine garrisons the cult spread
to German and Gaulish tribes around, finding perhaps some
native Triad of Goddesses with which it amalgamated,
while in Britain it remained, for the most part, confined
within its military habitat.[1]

III. Foreign cults were also imported into Britain from
non-Celtic sources. But these were confined to the haunts
of soldiers almost more rigidly than the Mother Goddesses.
One group, in its way an interesting group, consists of
Teutonic cults brought over by German soldiers serving in
the northern British frontier garrisons. Sometimes these
Germans accepted the gods whom they found in their new
quarters ; thus, a little band of men who bear German names
and expressly call themselves ' Germani ', is found erect-
ing an altar to Maponus close by the Roman Wall. But
often they kept to their Teutonic deities—Mars Thingsus
and the Two Alaisiagae, Garmangabis, Viradecthis, the
Unseni Fersomari, and many more. One German cult even
spread a little, though not beyond military surroundings.
The small ill-cut altars inscribed *deo Hveteri* or *Vheteri* or
Veteri were, as it appears, originally set up to a German god
Veter. Soon the worshippers forgot this and took the dedi-
cation to mean ' to the old god ' ; they even put it into the
plural and paid honour to the *di veteres*, the Old Gods
generally.[2]

[1] See Ihm, *Bonner Jahrbücher,* lxxxiii. 1–200, and my paper in *Archaeol.
Aeliana*, xv. 314. Including the kindred Suleviae, &c., about 60
examples have been found in Britain; of these the civilian districts
furnish barely a sixth—Cirencester 3, London 2 or 3, Colchester,
Bath, and Lincoln, 1 each ; at Lincoln, as once or twice elsewhere in
Celtic lands, Matres have been latinized into Parcae. A fourth Cirencester monument, which has usually been associated with the Mother
Goddesses, should probably be interpreted otherwise ; see *Archaeologia*,
lxix. 204 ff.

[2] See my note on *Eph. Epigr.* ix. 1182. The spelling *vhe-* or *hve-*
seems decisive of a Teutonic origin. The name is often written with
an *i* for one or both of the *e*'s.

Far more momentous to the Empire as a whole than these little Teutonic cults were the immigrant religions from the east, the worships of Mithras and Dolichenus and Cybele and Isis and others. They were very powerful. But in the Atlantic provinces, in Spain and western Gaul and Britain, their power was limited. They were confined to special areas, and in particular to military areas. Mithraism, the greatest of them all, overran Italy and central Europe and the Rhone valley which so closely copied Italy. But further west and north it went only where the troops went—to the Rhine frontier, to northern Britain, to the legionary fortresses. From Gibraltar to Fifeshire, barely half a dozen Mithraic monuments have been recorded which are not connected with the presence of soldiers. The cult of the Semitic Dolichenus was equally widespread in Italy and middle Europe and equally absent from Spain and from all but the military districts of Gaul and Britain. The barbaric rites of Cybele, although (perhaps in mitigated form) they invaded southern Gaul, were abhorred in the west and above all in Britain.[1] If we would find eastern cults in Britain, we must go to the military posts. At Corstopitum on the Tyne, just south of the Wall, was a military dépôt with some sort of settlement round it, where all manner of military men collected. There altars were set up to Astarte (Ashtoreth), to Heracles of Tyre, to Dolichenus, to Sol Invictus, to Panthea (Isis ?), as well as to the British Brigantia and Maponus and the German Veter. Nothing of the sort occurs in the towns or country-houses of southern Britain. Here, again, the influence of the Roman garrisons in Britain was limited to themselves (p. 26).[2]

---

[1] A. v. Domaszewski, *Journal of Roman Studies*, i. 54 ; Roscher's *Lex. Mythol.* s.v. Meter, 2927. A statue from Chesters (*Lapid. Sept.* 149) is often said to represent Cybele, but it is doubtful.

[2] Statuettes, figurines and other small objects connected with Oriental cults occur, of course, far beyond the limits noted in the text. But, so far as they were not mere curios, they point mainly to isolated worshippers.

FIG. 26. RELIEF OF DIANA AND HOUND FROM NETTLETON. (P. 73.)
(From a photograph.)

FIG. 27. RELIEF OF MERCURY IN FULL ROMAN STYLE WITH
A CELTIC GODDESS, FROM GLOUCESTER. (P. 73.)
(From a photograph.)

In Britain, therefore, as in other western lands, Romanization in religion meant, within the military area, a *sentina numinum*, a kitchen-midden of all sorts of cults heaped up from all quarters of the Empire. Outside that area it meant a mixture of Roman and native deities. The proportions of the mixture no doubt varied, as I have said above (p. 21). But we find little, if anything, to suggest that non-Roman elements were consciously preserved as being non-Roman. Even in the countryside, even in the shrines with 'Celtic' plans (p. 36), dedications are uniformly couched in Latin. At Nettleton, ten miles north-east of Bath, chance finds seem to have revealed a 'Celtic' temple with two reliefs of Diana.[1] Both were fully Roman in style (Fig. 26). Though no inscription survives to illuminate the cult, we need not doubt that here the passers-by—whether they knew it or not—worshipped Diana of the Romans. At Lydney, in the sanctuary of the Celtic god Nodens (p. 70), the temple-plan is Roman, the *graffiti* are in Latin, and a representation of Nodens himself (as it seems) might pass for a rude sketch of Neptune.

In all such cases Roman and native seem to be harmoniously intertwined, but the Roman is supreme. It was, no doubt, limited; the mixture included, as a rule, only a few of the Roman dominant gods. But it may be worth adding that, while in northern Gaul a Roman god sometimes appears along with a distinct Celtic companion, Mercury (for instance) with Rosmerta, that particular manner of mixing Roman and native is rarer in Britain.[2] Here the native element asserted itself less definitely beside the Roman. Now and then it occurs, as on a relief found in Gloucester [3] (Fig. 27), on which Mercury stands beside a goddess who seems not to be Rosmerta but some other Celtic deity.

---

[1] *Proc. of Bath and Distr. Branch of Somersets. Arch. and Nat. Hist. Soc.*, 1914, pp. 50 f.
[2] Cf. Jullian, *Hist. de la Gaule*, vi. (1920), 38, 48.
[3] *Catal. of Museum formed at Gloucester . . .* 1860, p. 8.

CHAPTER VIII

CHRONOLOGY OF THE ROMANIZATION

FROM the survey of the evidence which illustrates the Romanization of Britain, I pass to inquire how far history helps us to trace the chronology of the process. A few facts and probabilities emerge.

Intercourse between Britain and the Roman world began when Caesar conquered Gaul. It had lasted nearly a century when Claudius invaded the island in A.D. 43. During that age south-eastern Britain learnt much from Rome. Latin words, as I have said above (p. 29), now appeared on British coins. Arretine ware found its way, at least in stray pieces, to London (or Southwark), to Colchester, to Foxton in Cambridgeshire, to Alchester in Oxfordshire, to Purbeck in Dorset and some similiar sites, and it was well known and freely used at Silchester; the tribal capital of the Atrebates, which grew into the Romano-British Calleva, must have undergone some sort of Romanization long before A.D. 43.[1] The establishment of a Roman *municipium* at Verulam (St. Albans) before A.D. 60, and probably before A.D. 50,[2] points the same way. For the status of *municipium* was granted in the earlier Empire especially to native provincial towns which had, so to say, Romanized themselves, without Roman official action or official settlement of Roman soldiers or citizens, and had thus merited municipal privi-

[1] For Southwark and London see *Journal of Roman Studies*, i. 146 ; the account of the Southwark piece by Walters, *Proc. Cambridgeshire Antiq. Soc.* xii. 107, is incorrect. The total amount of Arretine found in London is small compared with that from Silchester and suggests that pre-Roman London (? Southwark) was unimportant. For Foxton see Babington, *Anc. Cambridgeshire*, p. 64. For Alchester see my note *Proc. Soc. Antiq. Lond.* xxi. 461.

[2] It is very much more suitable to Claudius than to Nero, and more suitable to the earlier than to the later years of Claudius.

leges.   It is quite likely that such Romanization had com-
menced at Verulam before the Claudian conquest and formed
the justification for the early grant.

After the conquest, the lowlands as far west as Exeter and
Shrewsbury, and as far north as the Humber, were subdued
by A.D. 50.   Romanization may therefore have marched on at
once.   About A.D. 60 certainly, the insurgent Britons under
Boudicca (Boadicea) were able to massacre an enormous
number of Romans and ' friendlies '—a number estimated at
the time as 70,000—and many of the victims must have
been Romanized Britons ; not impossibly this disaster
arrested awhile the civilizing process. The real advance came
a little later, in the Flavian period (A.D. 70–95).   Then
Roman culture spread in many provinces.   In Britain, towns
like Silchester, Caerwent, Wroxeter,[1] now take definite
shape, perhaps with official encouragement ; now, as we
may conjecture, tribal capitals were deliberately converted
into civilized towns, with street-plans and public buildings
of Roman type.   Now, too, the spa at Bath developed.[2]
Now, as Tacitus tells us, Latin began to be spoken, the toga
to be worn, temples, town-halls and private houses to be put
up in Roman fashion.   Now also civil judges, *legati iuridici*,
were appointed, presumably to deal with litigation arising
out of the advancing civilization.[3]   Tacitus states that
Agricola, as governor in Britain in 78–85, openly encouraged
this Romanization, and that his efforts met with great

---

[1] Silchester was plainly laid out all at once, and though it certainly
existed in some form long before A.D. 70, the evidence of coins and
pottery implies that it took a big step forward soon after 70 ; we may
connect that step with the laying out.   At Caerwent and Wroxeter,
coins, pottery and brooches suggest that there was little, if any, town
life before the Flavian age and a good deal soon after.

[2] At Bath the earliest datable stone belongs to A.D. 76, just before
Agricola came out (*Vict. Hist. Somerset*, i. 222, 269 ; *Eph. Epigr.*
ix. 996).

[3] A. v. Domaszewski, *Rhein. Mus.* xlvi. 599 ; C.I.L. ix. 5533, inscr. of
Salvius Liberalis, iii. 2864–9960, inscr. of Iavolenus Priscus, both of
the Flavian period.

success. We know, however, that the movement began before
he reached Britain, and it would seem that he was rather
carrying out the policy of his age than his own. Anyhow,
the policy succeeded. In A. D. 85 it was thought safe to
reduce the garrison of the province by a legion and some
' auxilia '—perhaps a quarter or a fifth of its hitherto
strength.[1]

Of further progress during the second century we have
little exact information. On the one hand we find that
serious risings vexed northern Britain at four points in this
century; about 115=120, again about 142, when the Scottish
Wall was built; yet again about 155=168,[2] and once more
about 175=180, when Caledonia was abandoned. So too
the years which ended the second and opened the third
century were full of trouble. All this must have kept even
the civilian area somewhat in disturbance. It was perhaps
at some crisis in this period that the flourishing county-town
of Isurium, a dozen miles north of York, had to shield
itself with stone wall and ditch.[3] On the other hand, the
development of the countryside by means of farms and
country-houses must have already begun. We meet early
traces of it in Kent and the south-eastern part of the island
generally, and sometimes outside these limits. Even in
Oxfordshire a site such as Northleigh (p. 41) has yielded
pottery which can hardly be later than the first half of the
second century. Even in the villages excavated by Pitt-
Rivers (p. 55), the use of Samian ware had spread before the
end of the first century.

Peace certainly set in after the opening of the third century. It was then, I think, that country-houses and farms

[1] *Classical Review*, 1904, p. 458 ; 1905, p. 58, withdrawal of Batavian
cohorts. The withdrawal of Legio II Adiutrix is well known.

[2] *Archaeologia Aeliana*, xxv. (1904) 142=7 ; *Proc. Soc. Antiq. Scotland*,
xxxviii. 454.

[3] The town-wall of Isurium, partly visible to-day, is built in a fashion
which suggests the second century rather than the late third or the
fourth century, when most of the town-walls in Britain and Gaul
were probably put up. Thus, its masonry shows the ' diamond
broaching ' which also occurs on the Wall of Pius in Scotland and
which must have therefore been in use during the second century.

became common in all parts of the civilized area. The statistics of datable objects discovered in these buildings seem conclusive on this point. Except in the south-eastern region, coins and pottery of the first century are infrequent, and many sites of rural dwellings have yielded nothing earlier than about A. D. 250. Despite the ill name that attaches to the third and fourth centuries, they were perhaps for Britain, as for parts of Gaul,[1] a period of progressive prosperity. Certainly, the number of British country-houses and farms inhabited during the years A. D. 280-350 must have been very large. Prosperity culminated, it seems, in the Constantinian Age. Then, as Eumenius tells us, skilled artisans abounded in Britain far more than in Gaul, and were fetched from the island to build public and private edifices as far south as Autun.[2] Then, also, and, indeed, as late as 360, British corn was largely exported to the Rhine Valley,[3] and British cloth earned a notice in the eastern Edict of Diocletian.[4] The province at that time was a prosperous and civilized region, where Latin speech and culture might be expected to prevail widely.

No golden age lasts long. In 343 Constans had to cross the Channel and repel the Picts and other assailants.[5] After 360 such aid was more often and more urgently required.

[1] Mommsen, Röm. Gesch., v. 97, 106, and Ausonius, passim. For evidence of active trade relations between the two countries see an interesting inscription discovered recently at Bordeaux (Comptes Rendus de l'Acad. des inscr. et Belles Lettres, 1921, p. 360).

[2] Eumenius, Paneg. Constantio Caesari, 21 civitas Aeduorum : : : plurimos quibus illae provinciae (Britain) redundabant accepit artifices, et nunc exstructione veterum domorum et refectione operum publicorum et templorum instauratione consurgit.

[3] Ammianus, xviii. 2, 3 annona a Brittaniis sueta transferri ; Zosimus, iii. 5.

[4] Edict. Diocl. xix. 36. Compare Eumenius, Paneg. Constantino Aug. 9 pecorum innumerabilis multitudo : : : onusta velleribus, and Constantio Caesari, 11 tanto laeta munere pastionum. Traces of dyeing works have been discovered at Silchester (Archaeologia, liv. 460, &c.) and of fulling in rural dwellings at Chedworth in Gloucestershire; Darenth in Kent, and Titsey in Surrey (Fox, Archaeologia, lix. 207).

[5] Ammianus, xx. 1. The expedition was important enough to be recorded on coins which show Constans on a galley, recrossing the Channel after his victory (Cohen, 9-13, &c.). On the history of the whole period for Britain see Cambridge Medieval History, i. 378.

Significantly enough, the lists of coins found in some country-houses close about 350–60, while other houses remained occupied till about 385 or even later. The rural districts, it is plain, began then to be no longer safe ; some houses were burnt by marauding bands, and some abandoned by their owners.[1] In the crisis of 367–8 the ravages seem to have spread over almost all the lowlands.[2] Therewith came necessarily, as in many other provinces, a decline of Roman influences and a rise of barbarism. Men took the lead who were not polished and civilized Romans of Italy or of the provinces, but warriors and captains of warrior bands. The Menapian Carausius, whatever his birthplace,[3] was the forerunner of a numerous class. Finally, the great raid of 406–7 and its sequel severed Britain from Rome. A wedge of barbarism was driven in between the two, and the central government, itself in bitter need, ceased to send officers to rule the province and to command its troops. Britain was left to itself. Yet even now it did not seek separation from Rome. All that we know supports the view of Mommsen. It was not Britain which broke loose from the Empire, but the Empire which gave up Britain.[4]

---

[1] See, for example, the coin-finds of the country-houses at Thruxton, Abbots Ann, Clanville, Holbury, Carisbrooke, &c., in Hampshire (*Vict. Hist. Hants*, i. 294 foll.). The Croydon hoard, deposited about A.D. 351 (*Numismatic Chronicle*, 1905, p. 37) may be due to the same cause.

[2] Ammian, xxvii. 8. 6.

[3] It is hard to believe him Irish (Rhŷs, *Cambrian Archaeol. Assoc.*, *Kerry Meeting*, 1891). The one ancient authority, Aurelius Victor (xxxix. 20), describes him simply as *Menapiae civis*. The Gaulish Menapii were well known ; the Irish Menapii were very obscure, and the brief reference can only denote the former.

[4] Mommsen, *Röm. Gesch.*, v. 177. Zosimus, vi. 5 (A.D. 408), in a puzzling passage describes Britain as revolting from Rome when Constantine III was tyrant (A.D. 407–11). It is generally assumed that when Constantine failed to protect these regions, they set up for themselves, and in that troubled time such a step would be natural enough. But Zosimus, a little later on (vi. 10, A.D. 410), casually states, in the middle of a chapter about Italy, that Honorius wrote to Britain, bidding the provincials defend themselves, so that the act of 408 cannot have been final. Possibly, however, as the context suggests

Such is, in brief, the positive evidence, archaeological, linguistic, and historical, which illustrates the Romanization of Britain. The conclusions which it allows seem to be two. First and mainly : the Empire did its work in our island as it did generally on the western continent. It Romanized the province, introducing Roman speech and town-life and culture. Secondly, this Romanization was not uniform throughout all sections of the population. Within the lowlands the result was on the whole achieved. In the towns and among the upper class in the country Romanization was substantially complete—as complete as in northern Gaul, and possibly even more complete. But both the lack of definite evidence and the probabilities of the case require us to admit that the peasantry may have been less thoroughly Romanized. It was covered with a superimposed layer of Roman civilization. But beneath this layer the native element may have remained potentially, if not actually, Celtic, and in the remoter districts the native speech must have lingered on, like Erse or Manx to-day, as a rival to the more fashionable Latin. How far this happened within the civilized lowland area we cannot tell. But we may be sure that the military region, Wales and the north, never became thoroughly Romanized, and Cornwall and western Devon also lie beyond the pale (p. 24, note 3). Here the Britons must have remained Celtic, or at least capable of a reversion to the Celtic tradition. *yeh man!*

and as Gothofredus and others have thought, the name ' Britain ' is here a copyist's mistake for ' Bruttii '. In any case the ' groans of the Britons ' recorded by Gildas, show that the island looked to Rome long after 410. On Constantine see Freeman, *Western Europe in the Fifth Century*, pp. 48, 148, and Bury, *Life of St. Patrick*, p. 329.

CHAPTER IX

The Sequel, the Celtic Revival in the Later Empire

So far we have considered the province of Britain as it was while it still remained in real fact a province. Let us now turn to the sequel and ask how it fits in with its antecedents. The Romanization, we find, held its own for a while after 400. The sense of belonging to the Empire had not quite died out even in sixth-century Britain. Roman names continued to be used, not exclusively, but freely enough, by Britons. Roman 'culture words' seem to occur in the later British language, and some at least of these may be traceable to the Roman occupation of the island. Roman military terms appear, if scantily. Roman inscriptions are occasionally set up. The Romanization of Britain was plainly no mere interlude, which passed without leaving a mark behind.[1] But it was crossed by two hostile forces, a Celtic revival and an English invasion.

I. The Celtic revival was due to many influences. We may find one cause for it in the Celtic environment of the province. After 407 the Romanized area was cut off from Rome. Its nearest neighbours were now the less-Romanized Britons of districts like Cornwall and the foreign Celts of Ireland and the north. These were weighty influences in favour of a Celtic revival. And they were all the more potent because, in or even before the period under discussion, the opening of the fifth century, a Celtic migration seems to have set in from the Irish coasts. The details of this migra-

---

[1] Much of the ornamentation used by post-Roman Celtic art comes from Roman sources, in particular the interlaced or plaitwork, which has been well studied by Mr. Romilly Allen. But how far it was borrowed from Romano-British originals and how far from similar Roman provincial work on the Continent, is not very clear (see p. 45).

tion are unknown, and the faint traces which survive of it are not altogether intelligible. The principal movement was that of the Scotti from North Ireland into Caledonia, with the result that, once settled there, or perhaps rather in the course of settling there, they went on to pillage Roman Britain. There were also movements in the south, but apparently on a smaller scale and a more peaceful plan.[1] At a date given commonly as A. D. 265–70—though there does not seem to be any very good reason for it—the Dessi or Déisi were expelled from Meath and a part of them settled in the south-west of Wales, in the land then called Demetia. This was a region which was both thinly inhabited and imperfectly Romanized. In it fugitives from Ireland might easily find room. The settlement may have been formed, as Professor Bury suggests, with the consent of the Imperial Government and under conditions of service. But we are entirely ignorant whether these exiles from Ireland numbered tens or scores or hundreds, and this uncertainty renders speculation dangerous. If the newcomers were few and their new homes were in the remote west beyond Carmarthen (Maridunum), formal consent would hardly have been required. Other Irish immigrants probably followed. Their settlements were apparently confined to Cornwall and the south-west coast of Wales, and their influence may easily be overrated. Some, indeed, came as enemies, though perhaps rather as enemies to the Roman than to the Celtic elements in the province. Such must have been Niall of the Nine Hostages, who was killed—according to the

---

[1] Rhŷs, *Cambrian Archaeol. Assoc., Kerry Meeting*, 1891, and *Celtic Britain* (ed. 3, 1904, p. 247), minimizes the invasions of southern Britain (Cornwall and Wales). Bury (*Life of St. Patrick*, p. 288) emphasizes them ; see also Zimmer, *Nennius Vindicatus*, pp. 84 foll., and Kuno Meyer, *Cymmrodorion Transactions*, 1895–6, pp. 55 foll. The decision of the question seems to depend upon whether we should regard the Goidelic elements in western Britain as due in part to an original Goidelic population or ascribe them wholly to Irish immigrants. At present, philologists do not seem able to speak with certainty on this point. But the evidence for some amount of invasion seems adequate. Cf. W. J. Ferrar, *London Quarterly Rev.*, April 1922, p. 189 foll.

traditional chronology—about A. D. 405 on the British coast and perhaps in the Channel itself.

All this must have contributed to the reintroduction of Celtic national feeling and culture.   A Celtic immigrant, it

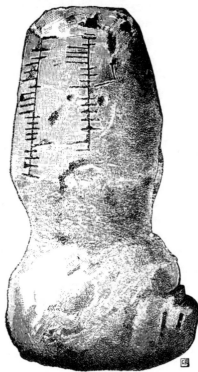

FIG. 28.   OGAM INSCRIPTION
FROM SILCHESTER.

may be, was the man who set up the Ogam pillar (Fig. 28), which was discovered at Silchester in the excavations of 1893.[1]   The circumstances of the discovery show that this pillar belongs to the very latest period in the history of Calleva.   Its inscription is Goidelic: that is, it does not belong to the ordinary Callevan population, which was presumably Brythonic.   It may be best explained as the work of some western Celt who reached Silchester before its British citizens abandoned it. We do not know the date of that abandonment, though we may conjecturally put it before, and probably a great many years before, A. D. 500.   In any case, an Ogam monument had

---

[1] *Archaeologia*, liv. 233, 441 ; Rhŷs and Brynmor Jones, *Welsh People*, pp. 45, 65 ; *Victoria Hist. of Hampshire*, i. 279 ; *English Hist. Review*, xix. 628.   Whether the man who wrote was Irish or British, depends on the answer to the question set forth in the preceding note. Unfortunately, we do not know when the Ogam script came first into use.   Professor Rhŷs tells me that the Silchester example may quite conceivably belong to the fifth century.

been set up before it occurred, and the presence of such an object would seem to prove that Celtic things had made their way even into this eastern Romanized town.

II. But a more powerful aid to the revival may be found in another fact—the destruction of the Romanized part of Britain by the invading Saxons. War, and especially defensive war against invaders, must always weaken the higher forms of any country's civilization. Here the assailants were cruel and powerful, and the country itself was somewhat weak. Its wealth was easily exhausted. Its towns were small. Its fortresses were not impregnable. Its leaders were divided and disloyal. Moreover, the assault fell on the very parts of Britain which were the seats of Roman culture. Even in the early years of the fourth century it had been found necessary to defend the coasts of East Anglia, Kent, and Sussex, some of the most thickly populated and highly civilized parts of Britain, against the pirates by a series of forts which extended from the Wash to Spithead, and were known as the forts of the Saxon Shore. Sixty or seventy years later the raiders, whether English seamen or Picts and Scots from Caledonia and Ireland, devastated the coasts and even the midlands of the province.[1] When, in the fifth century, the English came, no longer to plunder but to settle, they occupied first the Romanized area of the island. As the Romano-Britons retired from the south and east, as Silchester was evacuated in despair,[2] and Bath and Wroxeter were stormed and left desolate, the very centres of Romanized life were extinguished. Not a single one remained an inhabited town.

---

[1] About A. D. 405 Patrick was carried off from Bannavem Taberniae. If this represents the Romano-British village on Watling Street called Bannaventa, near Whilton in Northants (*Vict. Hist. Northants*, i. 186), the raids must have covered all the midlands : see *Engl. Hist. Review*, 1895, p. 711; hence Zimmer, *Realenc. für protestantische Theol.* x. (1901), Art. 'Keltische Kirche'; Bury, *Life of St. Patrick*, p. 322. There are, however, many uncertainties surrounding this question. Cf. Evans in *Num. Chron.*, 1915, p. 516.

[2] *Engl. Hist. Review*, xix. 625 ; *Vict. Hist. Hampshire*, i. 371-2; *Vict. Hist. Shropshire*, i. 217.

Destruction fell even on Canterbury, where the legends tell
of intercourse between Briton and Saxon, and on London,
where ecclesiastical writers fondly place fifth- and sixth-
century bishops. Both sites lay empty and untenanted for
many years.[1] Only in the far west, at Exeter or at Caerwent,
does our evidence not more or less forbid us to guess at
a continuing Romano-British life.

The same destruction came also on the population.
During the long series of disasters, many of the Romanized
inhabitants of the lowlands must have perished. Many
must have fallen into slavery, and may have been sold into
foreign lands. The remnant, such as it was, doubtless
retired to the west. But, in doing so, it exchanged the
region of walled cities and civilized houses, of city life and
Roman culture, for a Celtic land. No doubt it attempted
to keep up its Roman fashions. The writers may well be
correct who speak of two conflicting parties, Roman and
Celtic, among the Britons of the sixth century. But the
Celtic element triumphed. Gildas, about A.D. 540, describes
a Britain confined to the west of our island, which is very
largely Celtic and not Roman.[2] Had the English invaded
the island from the Atlantic, we might have seen a different
spectacle. The Celtic element would have perished utterly :

[1] For how many years, it is not possible to say. In 601 Gregory
the Great, writing to Augustine, indicates London and York as the
most appropriate seats of the two chief English bishoprics (Bede,
Hist. Eccles. i. 29). It might be inferred that they were then the two
chief English towns. But that does not necessarily follow. Gregory
might have obtained the names ' Lundonia ' and ' Eburaca ' from the
Vatican lists of fourth-century diocesan cities. In 731, however, Bede
(*op. cit.* ii. 3) speaks of London as *multorum emporium populorum terra
marique venientium,* and that may be more than a mere echo of the
copia negotiatorum et commeatuum maxime celebre of Tac. *Ann.* xiv. 33.

[2] How much of Britain was still British when Gildas wrote, he does
not tell us. But he mentions only the extreme west (Damnonii,
Demetae) ; his atmosphere is Celtic, and his rhetoric contains no
reference to a flourishing civilization. We may conclude that the
Romanized part of Britain had been lost by his time, or that, if some
of it was still British, long war had destroyed its civilization. Unfortunately, we cannot trust the traditional English chronology of the
period. For the date of Gildas, see W. H. Stevenson, *Academy,*
October 26, 1895, &c. ; I see no reason to put either Gildas or any
part of the *Epistula* later than about 540.

the Roman would have survived.   As it was, the attack fell
on the east and south of the island—that is, on the lowlands
of Britain.   Safe in its western hills, the Celtic revival had
full course.

It is this Celtic revival which can best explain the history
of Britannia minor, Brittany across the seas in the western
extremity of Gaul.   How far this region had been Romanized
during the first four centuries seems uncertain.   Towns were
scarce in it, and country-houses, though not altogether
infrequent or insignificant, were unevenly distributed.   At
some date not precisely known, perhaps in the middle of the
third century, it was in open rebellion, and the commander
of the Sixth Legion, which was stationed at York, one
Artorius Justus, was sent with a part of the British garrison
to reduce it to obedience.[1]   It may therefore have been, as
Mommsen and Jullian think, one of the least Romanized
corners of Gaul ; in it the native idiom may have retained
unusual vitality.   Yet that native speech was not strong
enough to live on permanently.   The Celtic which is spoken
to-day in Brittany is not a Gaulish but a British Celtic ; it
is the result of British immigrants.   This immigration is
usually described as an influx of refugees fleeing from
Britain before the English advance.   That, no doubt, was
one side of it.   But the principal immigrants, so far as we
know their names, came from Devon and Cornwall,[2] and some

---

[1] C.I.L. iii. 1919 = Dessau 2770.   The inscription must be later than
(about) A.D. 200, and it somewhat resembles another inscription (C.I.L.
iii. 3228) of the reign of Gallienus, which mentions *milites vexill. legg. Ger-
manicianar. et Brittanicin. cum auxiliis earum.*   Presumably it is either
earlier than the Gallic Empire of 258–73, or falls between that and the
revolt of Carausius in 287.   The notion of O. Fiebiger (*De classium
Italicarum historia*, in *Leipziger Studien*, xv. 304) that it belongs to the
Aremoric revolts of the fifth century is, I think, wrong.   Such an
expedition from Britain at such a date is incredible.

[2] The attempt to find eastern British names in Brittany seems
a failure.   M. de la Borderie, for instance, thinks that Corisopitum (or
whatever the exact form of the name is) was colonized from Corstopitum (Corbridge on Tyne).   But the latter, always to some extent
a military site, can hardly have sent out ordinary *émigrés*, while the
former has hardly an historical existence at all, and may be an ancient
error for *civitas Coriosolitum* (C.I.L. xiii (1), p. 491).

certainly did not come as fugitives.   The King Riotamus who (as Jordanes tells us) brought 12,000 Britons in A.D. 470 to aid the Roman cause in Gaul, was plainly not seeking shelter from the English.[1]   We must connect him, and the fifth-century movement of Britons into Gaul, with the Celtic revival and with the same causes that produced, for instance, the Scotic invasion of Caledonia.

This destruction of Romano-British life produced a result which would be difficult to explain if we could not assign it to this cause.   There is an unmistakable gap between the Romano-British and the later Celtic periods.   However numerous may be the Latin personal names and ' culture words ' in Welsh, it is beyond question that the tradition of Roman days was lost in Britain during the fifth or early sixth century.   That is seen plainly in the scanty literature of the age.   Gildas wrote about A.D. 540, three or four generations after the Saxon settlements had begun.   He was a priest, well educated, and well acquainted with Latin, which he once calls *nostra lingua*.   He was also not unfriendly to the Roman party among the Britons, and not unaware of the relation of Britain to the Empire.[2]   Yet he knew

[1] Freeman (*Western Europe in the Fifth Century*, p. 164) suggested that a migration of Britons into Gaul had been in progress, perhaps since the days of Magnus Maximus, and that by 470 there was a regular British state on the Loire, from which Riotamus led his 12,000 men. Hodgkin (*Cornwall and Brittany*, Penryn, 1911) thought that the soldiers of Maximus settled on the Loire about 388, and that Riotamus was one of their descendants.   He quotes Gildas as saying that the British troops of Maximus went abroad with him and never returned. That, however, is a different thing from saying that they settled in a definite part of Gaul.   For this latter statement I can find no evidence, and the Celtic revival in our islands seems to provide a better setting for Riotamus.

If Professor Bury is right (*Life of St. Patrick*, p. 354), Riotamus had a predecessor in Dathi, who is said to have gone from Ireland to Gaul about A.D. 428 to help the Romans and Aetius.   Zimmer (*Nennius Vind.*, p. 85) rejects the tale.   But it fits in well with the Celtic revival.

[2] Mommsen, Preface to *Gildas* (Mon. Germ. Hist.), pp. 9–10.   Gildas is, however, more Celtic in tone than Mommsen seems to allow.   Such a phrase as *ita ut non Britannia sed Romania censeretur* implies a consciousness of contrast between Briton and Roman.   Freeman (*Western Europe*, p. 155) puts the case too strongly the other way.

substantially nothing of the history of Britain as a Roman province. He drew from some source now lost to us—possibly an ecclesiastical or semi-ecclesiastical writer—some details of the persecution of Diocletian and of the career of Magnus Maximus.[1] For the rest, his ideas of Roman history may be judged by his statement that the two Walls which defended the north of the province—the Walls of Hadrian and Pius—were built somewhere between A.D. 388 and 440. He had some tradition of a coming of the English about 450, and of a reason why they came. But his knowledge of anything previous to that event was plainly most imperfect.

The *Historia Brittonum*, compiled a century or two later, preserves even less memory of things Roman. There is some hint of a *vetus traditio seniorum*. But the narrative which professes to be based on it bears little relation to the actual facts ; the growth of legend is perceptible, and even those details that are borrowed from literary sources like Gildas, Jerome, Prosper, betray great ignorance on the part of the borrower.[2] We have got here a very long way beyond Gildas. He, after all, knew something of Maximus and understood (however dimly) the relation of Britain to Rome. The ' Historia ' goes altogether astray on both points. On the other hand, the native Celtic instinct is more definitely alive and comes into sharper contrast with the idea of Rome. Throughout, no detail occurs which enlarges our knowledge of Roman or of early post-Roman Britain.

The same features recur in later writers who might be, or have been, supposed to have had access to British sources. Geoffrey of Monmouth—to take only the most famous—

---

[1] Magnus Maximus, as the opponent of Theodosius, seems to have been damned by the Church writers. Compare the phrases of Orosius, vii. 35 (Theodosius) *posuit in Deo spem suam seseque adversus Maximum tyrannum sola fide maior proripuit* and *ineffabili iudicio Dei* and *Theodosius victoriam Deo procurante suscepit.*

[2] The story of Vortigern and Hengist now first occurs and is obvious legend. A prince with a Celtic name may have ruled Kent in 450. There were, indeed, plenty of rulers with barbaric names in the fourth and fifth centuries of the Empire. But the tale cannot be called history.

asserts that he used a Breton book which told him all manner of facts otherwise unknown. The statement is by no means improbable. But, for all that, the pages of Geoffrey contain no new fact about the first five centuries, which is also true.[1] From first to last, the Celtic tradition preserves no real remnant of recollections dating from the Romano-British age. Those who might have handed down such memories had either perished in wars with the English or sunk back into the native environment of the west.[2]

But we are moving in a dim land of doubts and shadows. He who wanders here, wanders at his peril, for certainties are few, and that which at one moment seems a fact, is likely, as the quest advances, to prove a phantom. It is, too, a borderland, and its explorers need to know something of the regions on both sides of the frontier. I make no claim to that double knowledge. I have merely tried, using such evidence as I can, to sketch the character of one region, that of the Romano-British civilization.

---

[1] Thus, he refers to Silchester, and so good a judge as Stubbs once suggested that for this he had some authority now lost to us. Yet the mere fact that Geoffrey knows only the English name Silchester disproves this idea. Had he used a genuinely ancient authority, he would have (as in other cases) employed the Roman name. Another explanation may be given. Geoffrey wrote in an antiquarian age, when the ruins of Roman towns were being noted. Both he and Henry of Huntingdon seem to have heard of the Silchester ruins, and both accordingly inserted the place into their pages.

[2] The English mediaeval chronicles have sometimes been thought to preserve facts otherwise forgotten about Roman times. So far as I can judge, this is not the case, even with Henry of Huntingdon. Henry, in the later editions of his work, borrowed a few facts from Geoffrey of Monmouth, which are wanting in his first edition (see the Hengwrt and All Souls MSS. ; the truth is obscured in the Rolls Series text, as I have pointed out, *Athenaeum*, April 6, 1901). He also preserves one local tradition from Colchester : otherwise he contains nothing which need puzzle any inquirer. Giraldus Cambrensis, when at Rome, saw some manuscript which contained a list of the five provinces of fourth-century Britain—otherwise unknown throughout the Middle Ages (*Archaeol. Oxoniensis,* 1894, p. 224).

INDEX

Aldborough (*Isurium Brigantum*), 24, 40, 61 *note*, 76.
Arretine ware, 19 ; in Britain, 74.
Avotis on moulds of Gaulish potters, 31.

Bannavem Taberniae and St. Patrick, 83.
Bath, 61, 75 ; the Bath Gorgon, 53.
Brislington (near Bristol), house at, 39.
Brittany, British migration to, 84.

Caerwent (*Venta Silurum*), 24, 42, 70 ; a cantonal capital, 60.
Canterbury, derivation of name, 60 ; deserted after the Roman period, 84.
Cantonal system in Gaul, 20 ; in Britain, 58 foll.
Carausius, birthplace, 78.
Castor ware, 49 foll.
Celtic art, 48, 80 *note*.
Celtic languages used in Gaul and Britain, 18, 31 foll.
Celtic type of temples, 37 ; of houses, 38 foll.
Christianity, its attitude to native languages, 19.
Clanville, house at, 39.
Cloth made in Britain, 77.
Coloni (rural), in Britain, 65.
Coloniae (municipalities), 15 ; in Britain, 57.
Corbridge, 72, 85 ; the Corbridge Lion, 53.
Corn exported from Britain to the Continent, 77.
Cornwall, Roman remains in, 24 *note*.

Deae matres, 70.
Demetrius of Tarsus at York, 34.
Dessi (Déisi) migrate from Ireland to Wales, 81.
Deus Veter, di veteres, perhaps Teutonic deities, 71.
Devonshire, Roman remains in, 24 *note*.
Din Lligwy (Anglesea), village at, 46.
Dragon brooches, 52.

Emigration from Italy into the provinces, 16.

Frilford (Berks), house at, 39.

Gaulish kingdom of A.D. 258–73, 17.
Gaulish language used under the Empire, 18.
Geoffrey of Monmouth, 87.
Gildas, 84, 86.
Glastonbury, pre-Roman lake-village near, 55.
Gloucester, *colonia*, municipal tiles, 57, 63 ; sculpture of Mercury found at, 73.
Goidelic elements in Britain, 81, 82.
Gorgon at Bath, 53.

Henry of Huntingdon, Hengwrt and All Souls MSS., 88 *note.*
Hesione and Hercules, 51.
Historia Brittonum, 87.
Houses in Roman Britain, their varieties, their relation to houses in
    north Gaul, Italy, &c., 37 foll.

Icinos, tribe-name perhaps used of chief town, 60.
Ickleton (Cambridgeshire), *graffito* at, 33.
Imperial domains in Britain, 64, 65.

Jerome (St.), cited, 18.

Kent, derivation of name, 85.

Late Celtic art, 48.
Latin used in the provinces, 18 ; in Britain, 29.
Leicester, *graffito* from, 32.
Leugae in Gaul, 17.
Lincoln, 57.
London—
    Pre-Roman inhabitation, 74, *note.*
    Size, 62.
    Constitution of town, 62.
    Latin spoken in, 32.
    Deserted after the Roman period, 84.

Magnus Maximus, fate of his army, 86 *note.*
Mars in Roman provincial religion, 69.
Mars Lenus sive Ocelus, 70.
Mercury in Roman provincial religion, 69.
Mercury and Rosmerta, 21, 73.
Mithraism, distribution in western Europe and Britain, 72.
Mosaic floors in Roman Britain, 44.

Nettleton (on the Fosse), shrine of Diana, 73.
New Forest ware, 48.
Nodens, Celtic deity of Lydney, 70, 73.
Northleigh (Oxon), house at, 41, 76.

Ogam at Silchester, 82.
Oriental worships in Britain, 72.
Orpheus on mosaic floors, not Christian, 45.

Pergamene style in the Roman provinces, 54 *note.*
Pitt-Rivers, excavations by, 45, 55.
Plaxtol (Kent), inscribed tiles at, 33.
Pompeian houses compared with British, 40, 42 *note.*
Punic language, used in Roman Africa, 18.

Ravenna Geographer, 60.
Religion, 21 ; in Britain, 68.
Riotamus, British chief in Gaul, 85.

Samian ware, 19, 54.
Seebohm's theory of the suffix ' ham ', 65 *note.*
Silchester—
    Name, 61, 88 *note.*
    Pre-Roman, 74.

Silchester—
    Imperial domains under Nero at, 65.
    Development as Romano-British town, 75 *note*.
    Houses in, 42, 64.
    Latin used in, inscribed tiles, 29 foll.
    Temples of, 37.
    Town-planning of, 43, 64.
    Dyeing works in, 77 *note*.
    Abandoned, 83.

Tanarus, supposed Celtic god, 69.
Temples in Britain, 36, 62, 73.
Town-planning in Roman Britain, 64.
Towns of Roman Britain, 57–65.
Traprain Law (Haddington), 47.

Veter (*Vheter*), *di veteres*, 71.
Vergil, tags from, known at Silchester, 30.
Verulamium, *municipium*, perhaps pre-Roman town, 57, 74.
Villages in Roman Britain, 45, 55.
Vinogradoff, 35, 66.
Vortigern and Hengist, 87.

Wales, Roman, 24, 46, 81.
Warwickshire, few Roman remains in, 27.
Wroxeter (*Viroconium Cornoviorum*), 24, 37, 61.

York, *colonia* and fortress, 26, 57.